The Goon Show was the great anarchical BBC radio show which dominated the humour of the 1950s. It was born on May 28, 1951, under the title *Crazy People*, and its stars were Michael Bentine, Spike Milligan, Harry Secombe and Peter Sellers. In June 1952 it was re-named *The Goon Show*, Bentine left the following November and the final programme 'The Last Smoking Seagoon' went on the air in January 1960.

These Milligan-selected episodes, broadcast between 1954 and 1956, reveal the brilliant creativeness of Milligan's scripts. He produced such wonderful characters as the redoubtable Eccles, the cardboard Bluebottle, the invincible Neddie Seagoon, the horrific Grytpype-Thynne, and the indescribable Henry Crun and Minnie Bannister. Harry Secombe was the hero Neddie Seagoon and Peter Sellers took on the lion's share of the funny voices.

And half an hour's madness would descend on the sleeping inhabitants of the British Isles.

PUBLISHER'S NOTE

The scripts which Spike Milligan has chosen for this volume—the first in a planned series which will undoubtedly supplant *Hansard*—were all broadcast between October 1954 and January 1956. Future volumes will continue to chart the glorious years when the Goons ruled England. At 9.00 p.m. on the 30th April of this year, the Goons were summoned to Camden Town to record a special 'Royal' Goon Show (the first for twelve years) for the BBC's 50th Anniversary. In a programme note for that broadcast, Con Mahoney, Head of Light Entertainment, Radio, wrote:

> Historians of the future will find it difficult to lay the responsibility for the Goons at any one doorstep. A Westminster hostelry, the Grafton Arms, could well at some time in the future carry a blue plaque to the effect that 'Goonery Was Brewed Here'.
> Spike Milligan was the presiding scriptural genius—although during the long life of the Goons both Eric Sykes and Larry Stephens wrote a number of episodes. And Spike, with fellow Thespians Peter Sellers, Harry Secombe and in the very early shows Michael Bentine, breezed life into the fantasies of Goonery.

We see no reason to disagree.

Readers who never heard the melodramatic, breathlessly urgent voice of Dick Barton Special Agent, or the seductively suede tones of the late George Sanders, may be puzzled by such 'voice' instructions as (*Barton*), and (*Sanders*), just as *we* were by (*Izzy*), (*Bogg*), (*Flowerdew*), etc. Others may be baffled by the synopses, which often bear little or no relation to the scripts that follow.

The scripts have been reproduced faithfully, complete with instructions for the sound effects (F.X.) and tapes (GRAMS.), which were always a highlight. Where a performer's name is indicated (Peter, Spike, etc.) rather than a character's, the performer was using his own voice.

We are grateful to the Goons for generously allowing us to use the doodles and drawings they did on the back of scripts, envelopes, etc., during rehearsals over the years and to Norma Farnes for her patient help.

GOONOLOGY
28 May, 1951   First series Crazy People with Michael Bentine
22 June, 1952   Re-titled The Goon Show
11 Nov., 1952   Michael Bentine leaves
28 Jan., 1960   Final programme . . . The Last Smoking Seagoon

THE
GOON SHOW
Scripts

Written and Selected by

SPIKE MILLIGAN

With drawings by

Peter Sellers

Harry Secombe

Spike Milligan

SPHERE BOOKS LIMITED
30/32 Gray's Inn Road, London WC1X 8JL

First published in Great Britain by The Woburn Press 1972
Copyright © Spike Milligan 1972

First Sphere Books edition 1973

ISBN 0 7221 6079 8

The publishers acknowledge with thanks
the co-operation of the BBC.

Acknowledgements
are due to Associated Newspapers Group Limited (*Daily
Mail* article); Times Newspapers Limited
(*The Sunday Times* and *The Times* articles);
Press Association (photograph of the Goons and Royal
Family); London Express News and Feature Services
(*Daily Express* article); Beaverbrook Newspapers and
Philip Oakes (*Books and Art* article); *Radio Times*
(Gale Pedrick's article and photograph: 'A Giggle of
Goons'); BBC Pictorial Publicity Department (photographs:
St. David's Day Broadcast; Special Goon Show Broadcast);
the BBC for permission to quote from their special 50th
Anniversary programme.
The drawings on pages 104, 108, 123 are by the late Larry Stephens.

TRADE
MARK

Edited by Jeremy Robson and Elizabeth Rose
Designed by Harold King and Felix Gluck

Printed in Great Britain by Hazell Watson & Viney Ltd, Aylesbury, Bucks

CONTENTS

FOREWORD
PETER SELLERS

Denis Bloodnok & Partner (Deceased)
Solicitors
COMMISSIONERS FOR MILITARY AND CIVIL OATHS.
THREATS ISSUED AND RECEIVED.
OLD PHOTOGRAPHS STORED.

1, Crooks Building, Mayfair, Camden Town

Dear Sir,

My client, Mr. Pewter Fentners, the well known actor and thing, has instructed me to issue writs of paper unless you are prepared to withdraw this publication which contains certain passages written to a Miss Minerva Bannister, and alludes to a salacious relationship between that good lady and a Mr. H. Crun. Any persons reading these passages (ahhn!) could be alarmed and woken up.

Unless something is done, either by sending certain monies to Mr. Pewter Fentners by way of compensation c/o my good self, or better still, direct to me, I shall be forced (ahhn!) to issue a military document of a disturbing nature.

Be warned sir, you are dealing with - um - er - anyway my brother is a wrestler and my aunt is a policeman.

Cordially, (ahhn!)

Yours,

Denis Bloodnok (Major)

MAJOR DENIS BLOODNOK
SFI and BAR

INTRODUCTION
SPIKE MILLIGAN

It seems a bit daft to ask me to write an introduction to this book, because basically it needs no introduction. So, let us go on to something else. It's a nice day today except that I hit my knee against the corner of a flower pot, which caused slight abrasion to the skin, about, I would say, a quarter of an inch from the Patella.

The Patella is the part of the knee which, in turn, is that join between the top half of the leg and the bottom half. I think it helps when bending down, to have the leg bend in the middle, because you can get to the ground much quicker that way.

Of course, dwarfs don't really need knees to bend their legs, because from where they are they are already kneeling down, standing up, if you understand what I mean, which goes to show how much there is behind a slight abrasion $1\frac{1}{2}''$ below the knee, which is just above the Patella.

My mother bakes very good cakes, and sometimes lets us eat them; of course, if we don't eat them they get very stale, and we break them up and use them as humus to put in flower pots, on the edge of which I hit my leg this morning, so there. Please be more careful in future.

DAILY EXPRESS

MONDAY MAY 1 1972

The Goonpowder Plot

AS THE ROYALS MEET THE FAMOUS ECCLES AND Co.

Express Staff Reporter
JILL KING

Major Bloodnock, that supreme military idiot, lights the touchpaper and . . . BOOM! The Goons are back on the air.

Neddy Seagoon, Bluebottle, The Famous Eccles, Min and the villainous Moriarty....

Twelve years after all the old nonsense vanished, the three original Goons – Spike Milligan, Harry Secombe and Peter Sellers – got together again yesterday to record a new version.

An occasion not to be missed by Goon fans. And among the 500 who crowded into the little recording studio at the Camden Theatre, London, were Prince Philip, Princess Anne, Princess Margaret and Lord Snowdon.

Which was too good a chance for the Goons to miss....

"In the absence of Her Majesty", booms Secombe, "I'll be Queen."

Collapse of Princess Margaret in a fit of laughter.

Then a recording of Princess Anne's voice, with the sound of a galloping horse. . . .

It was a night which the greatest royal Goon fan, Prince Charles, had to miss with the greatest regret.

He is on duty with his ship, Norfolk, in the Mediterranean. And he sent a telegram which said:—

"Last night my hair fell out and my knees dropped off with envy when I thought of my father and sister attending the show."

When the Goon Show ended, and Bluebottle and Co. vanished for the last time, the royal party went back stage to meet the stars.

What about more Goon shows? Said Milligan: "No, I think it was a once only night. I'm ready for a wheelchair now. . . ."

The programme was recorded to be broadcast on Radio Four in October as part of the BBC's 50th anniversary celebrations.

So wait for it, kids. If you were too young to know the Beatles, at least you'll be able to stop asking Daddy: "Who WAS the Famous Eccles?"

Daily Mail

The Goons come back by Royal Appointment

VINCENT MULCHRONE at the Camden Theatre, London, last night. Prince Philip, Princess Anne and the Snowdons played themselves. The Queen was played by Harry Secombe.

ONLY the Goons could get away with it and, for the first time in 12 years, for one hilarious half-hour, the Goons were back together.

They passed through the time-slip with fantastic ease.

The genius behind the show, Spike Milligan, is now 53, Harry Secombe, 51, Peter Sellers, 47. Yet their humour is today's. Milligan was still writing it up till a few hours before the opening music.

The show opened with a telegram from a sailor who said that when he heard his father and sister were at the show "my hair turned green with envy and my knees fell off. I hope that one day you can give a show to a shipful of sea goons."

It was signed, simply, Charles.

Prince Charles, a Goon fan, is at present serving in HMS Norfolk, a guided missile destroyer in the Mediterranean.

Said the announcer: "As everybody who read the Isle of Arran Shoemakers' Monthly knows, Her Majesty the Queen was to have opened the Goon Show, but owing to a nasty rumour called Grocer Heath she has declined.

"However, at short notice, and wearing a floral cretonne frock, Mr Secombe has agreed to stand in for his Sovereign."

Secombe, all 16½st. of him, came in like a boxing MC. "Ladeez'n Gennlemen, my first impression as Queen will be a hedgehog doing an acupuncture on Yul Brynner's nut...."

The announcer broke in. "The coconuts were played at short notice by a young lady from Buckingham Palace."

(*True. Princess Anne clomped the coconuts in the recording studio before the show. It was her father's idea.*)

But, apart from tilts at the royal box, which was tilting with laughter itself, it was the old Goon Show, the purest form of surrealist humour on radio – or "talking-type wireless" as the Goons still prefer to call it.

They were all there, unchanged, instant immortals – the whingeing Bluebottle ("You filthy rotten swine, you") along with public school conman Hercules Grytpype-Thynne, Major Bloodnok and quavery Henry Crun – all played by Sellers.

Secombe was back to Neddie Seagoon and Milligan was the key figure, Eccles, the dimwit with the voice akin to Disney's Goofy....

The miracle was that in just eight hours of rehearsal yesterday they became the Goons again, sparkling and crackling, ad libbing to try to "throw" each other, changing lines in a flash, giving the old appearance of enjoying themselves even more than the audience....

The Goons used to be a show which, like *ITMA* before it – and Hancock and the satire boys afterwards – stopped the entire nation. It could do so again, even with jokes like:

How do you open a door?
Turn the knob on your side.
I haven't got a knob on my side.
On the door.

You have to hear it, as they say. Like Milligan singing, to the tune of *San Francisco* – "I left my teeth on Table Mountain, high on a hill, they smile at me ..."

It stirred many memories in me. I remember still the hunt for the Wild Christmas Pudding, found cowering in an African jungle, lashing its holly at anyone who approached.

Last night there was Westminster city council's plan for a rubbish dump skilfully situated in the middle of Hyde Park ....

Nothing, it seemed, had changed.

Ray Ellington was there, playing the gravel-voiced batman to Major Bloodnok, and Max Geldray with his harmonica.

By midnight, after a bit of a nosh with Royalty in the foyer of the old theatre where they recorded so many of their shows, the Goons were back on their separate paths.

Pity. With a bit of foresight, we could have imprisoned them in a luxurious studio for life so that their unique idiocy could sustain us in a world going crazy in quite a different way.

＊ ＊ ＊ ＊

THE TIMES

MONDAY MAY 1 1972

Goons let loose on air again

By Peter Waymark

The scene was the stage of the Camden Theatre in north London, where three of radio's greatest clowns had come together for the first time in 12 years to recreate that uniquely brilliant piece of nonsense, *The Goon Show*.

Reporter: I'm from *The Times*.

Spike Milligan: We can still be friends.

Another reporter: I'm from the *Today* programme.

Milligan: You are going to be late.

Question: What is it like doing *The Goon Show* again?

Harry Secombe (perspiring): Hysterical.

Question: What's the show about?

Secombe (thinks a moment): It's beyond description, really.

Question: What is the plot?

Secombe: We've never had a plot.

Milligan: I've got a plot, it's in Golders Green crematorium (blows raspberries, impersonates German officers, etc.).

The photographers gather round Peter Sellers, who stands on his head. "For the Australian papers", Milligan says. The Goons were back at the Camden, their old home, to record a special show for the BBC's fiftieth anniversary celebrations. It was a doubly nostalgic occasion, for the theatre is to be demolished soon.

Sellers (semi-seriously): "Coming back to it is like a strange dream, as though we had never parted. You know, our humour was really way ahead of its time. All those satire boys, *Beyond the Fringe*, *Private Eye*, they took on what we had started."

He said the new show would be as up to date as the audience would allow. "Naturally, they want to hear the old characters (does a bit of Bluebottle and a bit of Henry and Minnie), so it's a bit of the old and a bit of the new"

When the show was announced the BBC ticket unit was so flooded with applications that the 500-seat theatre could have been filled many times over. Tickets are said to have changed hands for £15. The lucky ones included the Duke of Edinburgh, Princess Anne, Princess Margaret and Lord Snowdon.

The script, written by Milligan and entitled, *The Goons' Benefit Night*, was in cracking form: "You can't tell the difference between a lump on the head and margarine? . . . the leadership of the Conservative Party is yours for the asking."

"There is a curse on the house of Moriarty? What is it? The Hampstead Building Society."

Other *Goon Show* veterans who assembled for the reunion included Ray Ellington, and Max Geldray, the harmonica player, flown in from the United States.

The Goons light up with leeks:
St. David's Day broadcast, 1956.
Left to right, Spike Milligan,
Peter Sellers, Harry Secombe.

Radio Times October 31, 1958

THE GOONS—as others see them

GALE PEDRICK *investigates the appeal of 'goonery' on*
the eve of the new series of shows starting this week
Home Service on Monday, with a repeat in the Light on Wednesday

IF, as some say, the outrageous, surrealist, inverted, unpredictable cartoons-in-sound of the Goons are an acquired taste, then it has been acquired by Royalty, statesmen, explorers, sportsmen, dons, film stars, and listeners under eighteen and over eighty.

Take the politician first, for it was a remark by Michael Foot which prompted me to find out how far indeed the Goons have cast their net.

'Spike Milligan is my favourite anarchist,' he said to me, 'in the most respectable way, of course, and I mean it as the highest possible tribute to the man. Indeed, the fact that the Goons are so popular is one of my hopes for the British public!'

'I was always a great fan of the Marx Brothers, and perhaps that has something to do with my admiration for the Goons. I'd like to think they'll last another hundred years!'

Royalty? Well, the Duke of Edinburgh heads the list. His choice of the Goons to act as his champions against the Cambridge University Tiddleywinks Club was a signal honour.

The Duchess of Kent and Princess Alexandra have more than once been to Goon recordings. Members of the recent Polar expedition laughed at the Goons amid the icy wastes of Antarctica and in their honour a special programme was written—showing how Seagoon set out to be the first man to play the bagpipes at the Pole.

Film stars? It seemed to me that Kenneth More might well be a Goon addict.

'You've come to the right man,' said Kenneth. 'I've been an honorary member of the Goon Club for nine years, and am terribly proud of it. It goes back to the time when I used to play Mr. Badger in *Toad of Toad Hall* and Harry Secombe was the Judge. Harry took me along to their favourite pub and the boys did their Goon act specially for me and my missus. I've adored their humour ever since.'

Bernard Miles told me he has offered the Goons his new Thames-side Mermaid Theatre for six weeks in which 'to do whatever they like.' 'The only precaution I shall take,' he said, 'is to put up iron railings at the river-end to protect the customers—and them.'

Why does Bernard like the Goons? 'Because their humour is so different from my own. Theirs is pure and inspired lunacy, but sometimes it takes a leap over the boundaries of lunacy and lands itself into staggering sense.'

To Bud Flanagan, leader of those Knights of Madness, The Crazy Gang, I said: 'You and your other clown princes started this sort of thing more than twenty years ago. What do you think?'

Bud was serious. 'I've followed the Goons ever since they started on the air—in fact I've watched their careers very carefully, and I'm one of their biggest champions. They're brilliant—especially Sellers. We're "crazy," but their humour is far more advanced than ours.'

The academic point of view? Alan Hale, president of the Students' Union, London School of Economics (Harry Secombe is a former vice-president), said: 'Apart from the subtle humour I find that students like the pace of these shows. It is so fast that you have to be pretty quick yourself to pick it up.'

It is so easy to say that Sellers, Secombe, and Milligan appeal to age and youth alike; but is it true? Here's my answer.

Ada Reeve, who by December will have been eighty years on the stage, told me: 'I'm pretty choosey, but you can quote me as saying that you can enjoy these young men at my age. Peter Sellers is a great artist, but I admire them all. They certainly make *me* laugh.'

Seventy-two years and five reigns younger is Master John Mitchell, 'Jennings' of the BBC's *Jennings at School*. He said: 'I think all schoolboys love the Goons because they're so funny. I know I always listen, and like all my friends I collect their records—and know all their famous sayings like "He's fallen in the water!"'

So, from schoolroom to Green Room, it will be 'welcome back!' to *The Goon Show* when it returns to the air on Monday.

THE SUNDAY TIMES
November 9, 1958

Surrealists in Sound

By SUSAN COOPER

IN a deserted London theatre on a grey Sunday afternoon the house-lights grow dim, and the built-out stage is festooned with microphone cables and wires looped from the roof. It is Goon time; they rehearse here at three.

Spike Milligan, Peter Sellers and Harry Secombe first gave humour another dimension six years ago, and the Goon Show now has a dedicated audience of over four million. They have just begun a new series of seventeen programmes, rumoured, as usual, to be the last; the Goons' relationship with the BBC is rather like a love affair, stormy with recurrent threats and frustrations but generally repaired in the end. For the Goon Show is the ultimate in pure radio.

Milligan, a loose-limbed Puck with a quick-silver smile and hair cut like a hearthrug, is the creator; five days a week he struggles to produce the script, and his partners do not properly become involved until five hours before the recording. Their own talents are channelled into films and the theatre, and they earn a great deal.

Before rehearsal Secombe announces diffidently that he has bought a Rolls-Royce. Sellers already has one, a gleaming brown giant parked outside the theatre. "That space behind it is for my Morris Minor," says Ray Ellington, the show's singer. "That little gap between the two," says Milligan, "is where I stand."

All Sunday afternoon they rehearse. Clowning, giggling, they work out the intricate sound-pattern, and Milligan, the perfectionist, constantly interrupts, gesticulating earnestly: "Jim, the atomic bomb's not loud enough. Louder, go on, till it gets to feedback point. . ."

Sellers, like a friendly businessman in his horn-rimmed glasses, sits drawing little Arabs on his script. "All the Goon characters are real, you know; William Mate, he's got a furniture shop near Spike's office . . . you go in and say: 'What sort of wood is this?' and he says: 'Solid wood, that is' . . . ."

AT thirty-three Sellers is the youngest Goon. Milligan is just forty; Secombe, ebullient and benign, is thirty-seven. Off stage, they are merely any group with a private joke, one of the secret vocabularies that children or lovers use. They call each other and everyone else "Jim", and Milligan adopts it as a label for himself in the script.

The lapses into Goon talk are those of the natural clown. Sellers turns his head to use a benzedrine inhaler and says politely: "Excuse me, will you, I've got the cringe." Secombe, asked after his health, says: "Absolutely first-class, my word yes," and goes off into the high-pitched cackle that is like a nervous tic.

After four hours the programme is ready; precision engineering in sound. The audience is let in, rustling with excitement; Milligan sits doodling at the piano, oblivious. Someone says: "He's winding down."

For fifteen minutes the Goons "warm up" the theatre; three astonishing young men whose talents brilliantly interact. Then the green light flashes over the clock, the announcer steps forward: "Recording in ten seconds from now," and the Goon Show has begun.

* *

Books and Art December 1957

GOONLAND IN DANGER

PHILIP OAKES *explores a comedy cult which tries to prove that 'nothing could be as mad as what passes for ordinary living'.*

THE MEADOW might be several degrees east of Stonehenge. There is a stream, a sinister cairn of stones, and a small gale is blowing. Through the tall grass trots a file of figures, like Druids on safari.

All of them wear long, shapeless nightgowns, and four of them are bent double under a grand piano. Behind them, the woods stand in deadly crescent.

Over the hill lies the end of the world. But their course is certain. They know what they have to do. Goons must always advance.

The Goon Show, boldly unveiled by the B.B.C. in 1952, and latterly translated into television, via 'The Idiot's Weekly' and 'A Show Called Fred', is more than a comedy cult. It is a state of mind, a commentary on the way we live, and a kind of genius.

Beamed on the personalities of its three stars—Peter Sellers, Harry Secombe and Spike Milligan; and the ingenuity of its two writers—Milligan again, and Larry Stephens—it has developed its own mythology, and created its own heroes, a suffering, surrealist band, gallant enough to turn Portland Place into a last barricade.

There is Major Dennis Bloodnok, an ex-Indian Army remittance man, seedy and impoverished beneath his solar topee; Neddie Seagoon, the ingenuous hero, with a maniacal laugh; Eccle, the teak-headed innocent; and Bluebottle, the minuscule plotter, dedicated to acts of unsuccessful sabotage.

The company also has its villains: Grytpype Thynne, the suede-voiced mastermind, and Count Jim Moriaty, a hatchet-

man in an astrakhan collar. And on the lunar fringe of the Goon world flit satellites such as Abdul the dragoman, and Henry Crun, a frail Victorian mouse.

'Lunacy is our planet,' says Spike Milligan. But it is lunacy of a purging and purposeful kind, that both reveals and releases.

Secure values

Chief begetter of the show, Milligan is an Irishman born of Indian Army parents. He looks back, not simply in anger, but with a pained regard that shreds the imperialist trappings of his childhood and seizes on the secure values of a not-so-distant past.

He hates the shoddy, the mean and the spurious, and his compassion extends to people like Colonel Redfern, in John Osborne's *Look Back in Anger*: 'a sturdy old plant left over from the Edwardian wilderness that can't understand why the sun isn't shining any more'.

But the compassion admits no sentimentality. 'My father believed in mowing down any black men who gave him trouble,' says Milligan. 'He was a good man. But he happens to have been criminally wrong.'

For Milligan, the Goon Show is an extension of his private view, something to defend against the ravages of conventional comedy. He is proud of his reputation as an innovator.

The compliment he values more than most was that paid by Bernard Levin in the *Manchester Guardian,* who claimed rhapsodically that the Goons had done for television what Gluck had performed for opera. 'That is,' he said, 'they have added a new dimension.'

After five years, Milligan still believes in the existence of other dimensions, but he seriously doubts whether he will be permitted to explore them. A brilliant, moody and difficult man, his relations with the B.B.C. have deteriorated into a smouldering truce.

This is partly due to Milligan's love of experiment, and the B.B.C.'s inability (or unwillingness) to assist him.

'Take the question of sound effects,' says Milligan. 'A lot of Goon comedy is pure sound—explosions, bullets whistling, feet clumping. You'd think the B.B.C. could cope with all that. They're supposed to have the greatest record library in the world.

'But d'you know what happened the other day? I wanted the sound of wolves howling, and I was told that the B.B.C. couldn't help. We finished up by doing the howling ourselves.'

Partners

As partners in an experimental comedy show, the Goons' solidarity has been threatened by their own success. After reaching stardom on the Goon Show, Harry Secombe was offered — and accepted — solo eminence on television. The career of Peter Sellers followed the same pattern, and he has just completed his first starring film part. Only Milligan has frightened off the big showmen.

He has been asked to write material for other comedians—and has refused. A well-known British film producer put forward the idea of a Goon film, and promised to arrange a lunch with Milligan within a few days to discuss the idea. Three months later, Milligan is still waiting.

Frustration

Blue-eyed, bearded and wearing the look of an Austrian Archduke expecting assassination, he ticks off his frustration as another man would count his assets. His spiritual home is a condemned garret.

In fact, he lives in a large Edwardian house in Finchley, where, propped up in bed at 4 p.m., he talked eagerly to me of the chemistry of Goon humour.

'Essentially,' says Milligan, 'it is critical comedy. It is against bureaucracy, and on the side of human beings. Its starting point is one man shouting gibberish in the face of authority, and proving by fabricated insanity that nothing could be as mad as what passes for ordinary living.'

Inspiration

Critics have detected the influence of Lewis Carroll, Lear, Stephen Leacock and James Joyce in the Goon scripts. (A long-time ambition of Milligan's has been to do a radio version of Joyce's *Ulysses*.)

But much of the inspiration comes from everyday newspaper reports. Milligan keeps a file, swollen with examples of factual Goon-type humour.

For example: 'Because birds have taken the straw from the roof of their thatched cottage at Otham, Kent, the occupants have had their rates reduced.'

From life

And again: 'Seventy-five-year-old Sir Rupert Shoobridge, former president of the Tasmanian Legislative Council, visiting Britain had a letter from home to say that a rat has eaten three of his suits, his top hat, evening dress and morning suit. Cancelling important farewell appointments, he rushed off to his Savile Row tailors to be fitted for replacements. "I would like to murder that rat," he muttered.'

Either item could slip naturally into a Goon Show. And it is quite likely that they will.

This year, Milligan continued with the Goon Show only at the insistence of the B.B.C. And next year may see its demise.

'The point is,' says Milligan, 'that it must continue to be experimental. And the support for the kind of experiments that I want to make simply isn't there.'

* * * * * * * * * * * * * * * * * * * *

SPIKE MILLIGAN

Born in 1918 in India, where his father was a soldier, Spike Milligan came to England in 1934. Early jobs ranged from factory hand to scrubber in a laundry; he was also a trumpet player in a band for a while, then a trumpet player not in a band. He met Harry Secombe in the army, teamed up for concerts, began to write, met Peter Sellers—and so began *The Goon Show*. Winner of the Producers' and Directors' 'Writer of the Year' award on several occasions, he has appeared in many films and starred in successful West End plays (*The Bed Sitting-Room*, *Oblomov*). His writings include the novel *Puckoon*, various books of children's and comic verse, and the best-selling *Adolf Hitler—My Part in His Downfall* (soon to be filmed by MGM).

HARRY SECOMBE

As a schoolboy in his native Wales, Harry Secombe was a popular 'turn' at church socials with his impersonations. After working as a pay clerk and completing war service, he took a job at the Windmill Theatre. It was there that he started to sing, and that the Sellers/Milligan/Bentine/Secombe association began. Since then he has achieved fame as a comedian and singer on both sides of the Atlantic. Star of many popular stage and screen musicals (including *Pickwick* and *Oliver!*), he last year celebrated 25 versatile years in show business.

Secombe, Milligan, Sellers.

PETER SELLERS

With both parents and eight uncles in show business, Peter Sellers's career was a foregone conclusion. After service in the RAF, he joined Ralph Reader's *Gang Show*, then got a job at the Windmill Theatre before being recruited by the BBC—who quickly recognized his extraordinary talents as a man of many voices. His film career, which has been as brilliant as it has been varied, began in 1954. Since his first key role (in *The Ladykillers*), many internationally famous films have followed, including *I'm All Right Jack*, *Dr. Strangelove*, *The Millionairess* and *There's a Girl in My Soup*. He has just finished filming *Alice in Wonderland*.

RAY ELLINGTON

An ex-RAF P.T. instructor, Ray Ellington formed his original Ray Ellington Quartet in 1950. He was known to millions through the radio programme *Mr. Ros and Mr. Ray* (in which he starred with Edmundo Ros), as well as through the Goon Shows. In 1970 he established the popular Ray Ellington Big Band and Singers.

WALLACE GREENSLADE

Wallace Greenslade ('Bill') joined the staff of the BBC in 1945 as a general announcer. In addition to his stoic appearances with the Goons, he worked on a wide variety of programmes until his death in 1961.

MAX GELDRAY

Jazz harmonica player Max Geldray was born in 1935 in Holland, where he began his career. After doing many broadcasts and playing in nightclubs all over Europe, he joined the Ray Ventura Band in France. In Paris he played with such jazz 'greats' as Django Reinhardt, who became a good friend. He settled in England after the war where he grew popular through his radio, TV and live performances, and such records as *Goon With The Wind*(!). He emigrated to America in 1962, and now works for the Christian Science Movement in California.

As a result of our demands for biographical data (and much original research) the following reactions were received and information obtained:

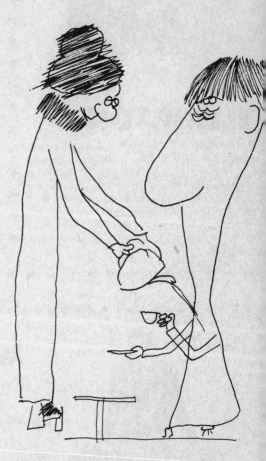

ECCLES
(The Original Goon)
Born 1863. Only child of Ethel Cox. Virgin birth. Educated at Convent till age 7 – end of education. Has had 18,312 interviews for jobs. Has never been employed. Spends his days walking around saying "Hello dere" to anyone who will listen. Wears a 33-year-old Burton suit. Is occasionally used by the Metropolitan Police for target practice. Was once painted by Augustus John from head to foot with whitewash. Likes children. Children like him. His economy drives consist of wearing only one sock. Was the personal friend of a brewer's dray. Was Home Secretary for 3 days – until the printing error was discovered. Lives near 29 Scrot Lane, Balham. Clubs: none. Recreations: walking around saying "Hello dere" to anyone who will listen.

BLUEBOTTLE
(A cardboard cut-out liquorice and string hero)
'Ye he he! Heuheuheuheuheu he!'
A proffered bag of dolly mixtures plus a free subscription to *Wonder Mag* persuaded the ragged Boy Scout with a penchant for Sabrina and an eye for the birds to append this, his signature, to the aforegoing:

NEDDIE SEAGOON
(True blue British idiot and hero always)
'What what what what what? Can't stop now – must dash to the last page.'
(A flash through this book revealed that Mr Seagoon had indeed dashed the last page.)

MR HENRY CRUN
(A thin ancient and inventor)
'Mnk – grnk – mnk – mnk – grmp.'
(Persistent questioning failed to refresh Mr. Crun's memory as to the identity of Mr Henry Crun, beyond the remark, 'Henry Crun? Mnk – isn't that the name of – mnk – Henry Crun?')

MISS MINNIE BANNISTER
(Spinster of the Parish)
Although she refused to be quoted directly, some Sanders-style flattery induced Miss Bannister to reveal that she had once danced the Can-Can at the Windmill Theatre, and that in the naughty nineties she had been 'the darling of Roper's Light Horse'. She also hinted at a former passionate involvement with a bounder named Bloodnok. When pressed, however, she screamed and referred all further questions to her spokesman and companion of honour, Mr Henry Crun.

COMTE TOULOUSE-MORIARTY OF THE HOUSE OF ROLAND
(French scrag and lackey to Grytpype-Thynne)
Born 1920 Paris. Educated – Sorbonne and St. Cyr Military Academy. Captained French Moron Racing Car Team at Brooklands 1927 – became the Latin darling of the Motoring Set, lionised by London, seen at all smart places – The Cafe Royal – the Ritz – danced the Tango all night long with Lady Astor. Operation for piles. Wall Street crash – family fortune decimated. Started work as a gigolo at New Cron Palais de Danse, was befriended by Hercules Grytpype-Thynne, who offered to 'manage' his career. Under Grytpype's careful 'management' he is now bald, daft, deaf, and worthless. Currently working under licence as a trainee corpse in Leith Crematorium and hoping to play the lead in *Jesus Christ Superstar*. Clubs: Chateau Neuf. Recreation: trying to escape.

HERCULES GRYTPYPE-THYNNE, THE HON.
(A plausible public school villain and cad)
Son of Lord "Sticky" Thynne and Miss Vera Colin, a waitress at Paddington Station. Educated at Eton Mixed Grammar School, Penge; was manager for the rugby team, 15th man at cricket, subject of a police investigation on school homosexuality. Eventually left school at 20 – did 2 years at Oxford, subject of a police investigation on homosexuality. Joined Household Cavalry; served throughout the war at Knightsbridge barracks. Subject of a military police investigation on homosexuality. Implicated in sale of Regimental Silver Plate – 3 years at the Scrubbs. Was subject of a prisoners' investigation on homosexuality. On release became a life member of Harrow Labour Exchange. Joined the Foreign Office – implicated in homosexuality with Masai goat herd. Roving Ambassador to the Outer Hebrides. Awarded OBE in Birthday Honours. Currently Private Secretary to a British Lord. Club: Junior Carlton. Recreations: Homosexuality.

MAJOR DENIS BLOODNOK, IND. ARM. RTD.
(Military idiot, coward and bar)

Born 1867 and 1880, Sandhurst NAAFI. Served in S. African war – taken prisoner on first day under strange circumstances. Released by Boers after 3 days as being "unreliable". Spent the rest of the war in the Pay Corps. Large sums of money were in his keeping. They were never traced. Transferred to Aldershot Southern Command as Quartermaster General – was responsible for 30,000 rupees,worth of stores. They were never traced. Military Police traced *him* to Rangoon, where he was found wearing false testicles in a Freak Show. Cashiered. Married the Hon. Mrs. Scrack-Thing. Divorced. Rejoined Army under an assumed height as Florence Bloodnok: served 1 year in ATS. His disguise became known when he reported a sailor for molesting him in an air-raid shelter. Using his position as a mason, he re-joined the Army as a Major; he saw action and suffered wounds in the bedroom of Mrs. Madge Feel. World War II – he was found hiding in a hut near Quetta, where he swore a solemn oath that he was an eccentric Hindu fakir who had gone white with fear. Cashiered for the 7th time – a world military record. Wearing a stocking mask, he rejoined the British Army as a Chinaman. Using masonic connections he became a Major again. Clubs: Anyone. Recreations: Piccadilly Circus. Hobbies: The Indian Army. Agent: Miss M. Bannister.

WILLIUM 'MATE' COBBLERS
(Drains cleared while you wait)

Born Shoreditch 1900, son of Fred "Chopper" Cobblers, OBE, road sweeper, and Vera Colin. Left school at 14. Joined Thomas Crapper & Son as tea boy. Joined Chislehurst Laundry as tea boy. Joined Woolwich Arsenal as tea boy. Conscripted for World War I as Private in Sappers and Miners as tea boy. Rose to rank of acting unpaid Lance Corporal – injured in action by tea urn falling on head. Mentioned in dispatches as "always moaning". Discharged in 1918, since when he has wandered the streets of London telling motorists, with no authority whatsoever, "You can't park there" or "Put that cigarette out" or "I don't know, I'm a stranger round here" or "Why don't you get yer 'air cut?" or "Two years in the army would do 'em good" or "Bloody foreigners" or "I spent 4 years fighting for this country." Now uniformed doorman at BBC Aeolian Hall, wears full war medals at all times, and King's badge for the disabled. Informs all visitors to the BBC, "It's nothing to do with me mate." Clubs: Bristol Legion. Recreations: saying "You can't park there", etc.

THE
SCRIPTS

THE DREADED BATTER PUDDING HURLER
(OF BEXHILL·ON·SEA)

The Goon Show: No. 102 (5th Series, No. 3)
Transmission: Tuesday, 12th October 1954:
8.30—9.00 p.m. Home Service
Studio: Paris Cinema, London

The main characters

Mr Henry Crun	Peter Sellers
Miss Minnie Bannister	Spike Milligan
Ned Seagoon	Harry Secombe
Lance Brigadier Grytpype-Thynne	Peter Sellers
Sergeant Throat	Spike Milligan
Major Denis Bloodnok	Peter Sellers
Eccles	Spike Milligan
Odium	Spike Milligan
Moriarty	Spike Milligan
Willium	Peter Sellers
Bluebottle	Peter Sellers

The Ray Ellington Quartet
Max Geldray
Orchestra Conducted by Wally Stott
Announcer: Wallace Greenslade
Script by Spike Milligan
Production by Peter Eton

How young Ned Seagoon was called in by the terrorised gentle-folk of Bexhill to help track down the dreaded Batter Pudding Hurler. Striking when least expected, the 'Hurler' caused such havoc during the blackout of 1941 that troops, massed against the German invasion, were ordered to join the hunt. A trail of cold Batter Puddings eventually led Ned Seagoon to North Africa where, with the aid of Major Bloodnok, he finally cornered the traitor...

BILL	This is the BBC Home Service.
F.X.	**PENNY IN MUG.**
BILL	Thank you. We now come to the radio show entirely dedicated to the downfall of John Snagge.
HARRY	He refers, of course, to the highly esteemed Goon Show.
GRAMS	**SORROWFUL MARCH WITH WAILS.**
HARRY	Stop! Time for laughs later — but now to business. Mr. Greenslade? Come over here.
F.X.	**CHAINS.**
BILL	Yes, Master?
HARRY	Tell the waiting world what we have for them.
BILL	My lords, ladies and other National Assistance holders — tonight the League of Burmese Trombonists presents a best-seller play entitled:
ORCHESTRA	**TYMPANY ROLL. HELD UNDER:—**
PETER	The Terror of Bexhill-on-Sea or . . .
ORCHESTRA	**THREE DRAMATIC CHORDS.**
HARRY	The Dreaded Batter Pudding Hurler.

ORCHESTRA	**CLIMAX. THEN DOWN NOW BEHIND:—**
BILL	The English Channel 1941. Across the silent strip of green-grey water — in England — coastal towns were deserted, except for people. Despite the threat of invasion and the stringent blackout rules, elderly gentlefolk of Bexhill-on-Sea still took their evening constitutions.
F.X.	**EBB TIDE ON A GRAVEL BEACH.**
CRUN	Ohhh — it's quite windy on these cliffs.
MINNIE	What a nice summer evening — typical English.
CRUN	Mnk yes — the rain's lovely and warm — I think I'll take one of my sou' westers off — here, hold my elephant gun.
MINNIE	I don't know what you brought it for — you can't shoot elephants in England.
CRUN	Mnk? Why not?

MINNIE	They're out of season.
CRUN	Does this mean we'll have to have pelican for dinner again?
MINNIE	Yes, I'm afraid so.
CRUN	Then I'll risk it, I'll shoot an elephant out of season.
BOTH	*(Go off mumbling in distance)*
BILL	Listeners who are listening will, of course, realise that Minnie and Henry are talking rubbish — as erudite people will realise, there are no elephants in Sussex. They are only found in Kent North on a straight line drawn between two points thus making it the shortest distance.
F.X.	**PENNY IN MUG.**
BILL	Thank you.
CRUN	. . . .well, if that's how it is I can't shoot any.
MINNIE	Come Henry, we'd better be getting home — I don't want to be caught on the beaches if there's an invasion.
CRUN	Neither do I — I'm wearing a dirty shirt and I — mnk — don't —
F.X.	**CLANK OF IRON OVEN DOOR.**
CRUN	. . . Minnie?
MINNIE	What what?
CRUN	Did you hear a gas oven door slam just then?
MINNIE	Don't be silly, Henry — who'd be walking around these cliffs with a gas oven?
CRUN	Lady Docker.
MINNIE	Yes, but apart from the obvious ones — who'd want to . . .
F.X.	**WHOOSH — SPLOSH — BATTER PUDDING HITTING MINNIE**
MINNIE	Ooooooooooooooohohohohohohohohohohohohohohohohohohoho . . .
CRUN	No, I've never heard of him.
MINNIE	Help, Henery — I've been struck down from behind. Helpp.
CRUN	Mnk — oh dear dear. *(Calls)* Police — English Police — Law Guardians???
MINNIE	Not too loud, Henry, they'll hear you.
F.X.	**POLICE WHISTLE.**
SEAGOON	*(approaching)* Can I help you, sir?
CRUN	Are you a policeman?
SEAGOON	No, I'm a constable.
CRUN	What's the difference?

SEAGOON	They're spelt differently.
MINNIE	Ohhhhhhhh.
SEAGOON	Oh! What's happened to this dear old silver-bearded lady?
CRUN	She was struck down from behind.
SEAGOON	And not a moment too soon — congratulations, sir.
CRUN	I didn't do it.
SEAGOON	Coward — hand back your OBE. Now tell me who did this felonous deed. What's happened to her?
CRUN	It's too dark to see — strike a light.
SEAGOON	Not allowed in blackout.
MINNIE	Strike a dark light.
SEAGOON	No madam, we daren't — why, only twenty-eight miles across the Channel the Germans are watching this coast.
CRUN	Don't be a silly-pilly policeman — they can't see a little match being struck.
SEAGOON	Oh, alright.
F.X.	MATCH STRIKING — QUICK WHOOSH OF SHELL — SHELL EXPLODES.
SEAGOON	Any questions?
CRUN	Yes — where are my legs?
SEAGOON	Are you now aware of the danger from German long-range guns?
CRUN	Mnk ahh! I've got it — I have the answer — just by chance I happen to have on me a box of German matches.
SEAGOON	Wonderful — strike one — they won't fire at their own matches.
CRUN	Of course not — now . . .
F.X.	MATCH STRIKING AND FLARING — WHOOSH OF SHELL — SHELL BURST.
CRUN	. . . Curse . . . the British!!!
SEAGOON	We tried using a candle, but it wasn't very bright and we daren't light it — so we waited for dawn — and there, in the light of the morning sun, we saw what had struck Miss Bannister. It was — a Batter Pudding.
ORCHESTRA	DRAMATIC CHORD.
CRUN	It's still warm, Minnie.
MINNIE	Thank Heaven — I hate cold Batter Pudding.
CRUN	Come, Minnie, I'll take you home — give you a hot bath — rub you down with the anti-vapour rub — put a plaster on your back — give your feet a mustard bath, and then put you to bed.

SEAGOON	Do you know this woman?
CRUN	Devilish man — of course I do — this is Minnie Bannister, the world-famous poker player — give her a good poker and she'll play any tune you like.
SEAGOON	Well, get her off this cliff, it's dangerous. Meantime, I must report this to the Inspector. I'll call on you later — goodbye.
F.X.	(PAUSE) DISTANT SPLASH.
SEAGOON	As I swam ashore I dried myself to save time. That night I lay awake in my air-conditioned dustbin thinking — who on earth would want to strike another with a Batter Pudding? Obviously it wouldn't happen again, so I fell asleep. Nothing much happened that night — except that I was struck with a Batter Pudding.
SPIKE	Mmmmm — it's all rather confusing, really.

BILL	In the months to come, thirty-eight Batter Puddings were hurled at Miss Bannister — a madman was at large — Scotland Yard were called in.
ORCHESTRA	LINK.
GRYTPYPE-THYNNE	*(Sanders throughout)* Inspector Seagoon — my name is Hercules Grytpype-Thynne, Special Investigation. This Batter Pudding Hurler —
SEAGOON	Yes?
GRYTPYPE-THYNNE	He's made a fool of the police.
SEAGOON	I disagree — we were fools long before he came along.
GRYTPYPE-THYNNE	You silly twisted boy. Nevertheless, he's got to be stopped — now, Seagoon —
SEAGOON	Yes yes yes yes yes yes?
GRYTPYPE-THYNNE	. . . Please don't do that. Now, these Batter Puddings — they were obviously thrown by hand.
SEAGOON	Not necessarily — some people are pretty clever with their feet.
GRYTPYPE-THYNNE	For instance?
SEAGOON	Tom Cringingknutt.
GRYTPYPE-THYNNE	Who's he?

SEAGOON	He's a man who's pretty clever with his feet.
TPYPE-THYNNE	What's his name?
SEAGOON	Jim Phlatcrok.
TPYPE-THYNNE	Sergeant Throat?
THROAT	Sir?
TPYPE-THYNNE	Make a note of that.
THROAT	Right. Anything else?
TPYPE-THYNNE	Yes.
THROAT	Right.
TPYPE-THYNNE	Good. Now Seagoon, these Batter Puddings — were they all iden⁺ cal?

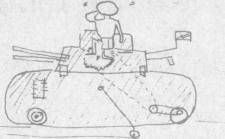

SEAGOON	All except the last one. Inside it — we found this.
TPYPE-THYNNE	Oh! An Army Boot! So the Dreaded Hurler is a military man. Any troops in the town?
SEAGOON	The fifty-sixth Heavy Underwater Artillery.
TPYPE-THYNNE	Get there at once — arrest the first soldier you see wearing one boot.
SEAGOON	Ying tong iddle I po.
TPYPE-THYNNE	Right — off you go.
ORCHESTRA	BLOODNOK SIGNATURE TUNE.
BLOODNOK	Bleiough — aeioughhh —bleioughhhh — how dare you come here to my H.Q. with such an —
SEAGOON	I tell you, Major Bloodnok, I must ask you to parade your men.
BLOODNOK	Why?
SEAGOON	I'm looking for a criminal.
BLOODNOK	You find your own — it took me years to get this lot.
SEAGOON	Ying tong iddle I po.
BLOODNOK	Very well then — Bugler Max Geldray? Sound fall in — the hard way.

MAX & ORCHESTRA	**THEY WERE DOING THE MAMBO** *(Applause)*
ORCHESTRA & CAST	*(Murmurs of distrust)*
BLOODNOK	Silence, lads! I'm sorry I had to get you out of bed in the middle of the day — but I'll see you get extra pay for this.
ORCHESTRA & CAST	You flat 'eaded kipper — Gawn, drop dead — I'll claht yer flippin' head — Gorn, shimmer orf.
BLOODNOK	Ahhhhhhh, that's what I like — spirit. Now, Seagoon — which is the man?
SEAGOON	I walked among the ranks looking for the soldier with one boot but my luck was out: the entire regiment were barefooted — all save the officers, who wore reinforced concrete socks.
BLOODNOK	Look Seagoon, it's getting dark. You can't see in this light.
SEAGOON	I'll strike a match.
F.X.	**MATCH . . . WHOOSH OF SHELL EXPLOSION.**
SEAGOON	Curse, I forgot about the Germans.
ECCLES	We want our beddy byes.
SEAGOON	Who are you?
ECCLES	Lance Private Eccles, but most people call me by my nick-name.
SEAGOON	What's that?
ECCLES	Hahum. Nick.
SEAGOON	I inspected the man closely — he was the nearest thing I'd seen to a human being, without actually being one.
BLOODNOK	Surely you don't suspect this man — why, we were together in the same company during that terrible disaster.
SEAGOON	What company was that?
BLOODNOK	Desert Song 1933.
SEAGOON	Were you both in the D'Oyly Carte?
BLOODNOK	Right in the D'Oyly Carte.
SEAGOON	I don't wish to know that, but wait!! At last — by the light of a passing glue factory — I saw that Eccles was only wearing — one boot!
ECCLES	Well, I only got one boot.
SEAGOON	I know — but why are you wearing it on your head?
ECCLES	Why? It fits, dat's why — what a silly question — why — why —
SEAGOON	Let me see that boot. *(Sotto)* Mmmm, size nineteen . . . *(Aloud)* What size head have you got?
ECCLES	Size nineteen.

SEAGOON	Curse — the man's defence was perfect — Major Bloodnok?
BLOODNOK	How dare you call me Major Bloodnok.
SEAGOON	That's your name.
BLOODNOK	In that case — I forgive you.
SEAGOON	Where's this man's other boot?
BLOODNOK	Stolen.
SEAGOON	Who by?
BLOODNOK	A thief.
SEAGOON	You sure it wasn't a pickpocket?
BLOODNOK	Positive — Eccles never keeps his boots in his pocket.
SEAGOON	Damn. They all had a watertight alibi — but just to make sure I left it in a fish tank overnight. Next morning my breast pocket 'phone rang.
F.X.	RING.
SEAGOON	Hello?
CRUN	Mr. Seagoon — Minnie's been hit with another Batter Pudding.
SEAGOON	Well, that's nothing new.
CRUN	It was — this one was stone cold.
SEAGOON	Cold???
CRUN	Yes — he must be losing interest in her.
SEAGOON	It proves also that the phantom Batter Pudding Hurler has had his gas-pipe cut off! Taxi!
F.X.	BAGPIPES. RUNNING DOWN.
SPIKE	Yes?

SEAGOON	The Bexhill Gas Works, and step on it.
SPIKE	Yes.
F.X.	**BAGPIPES. FADE OFF.**
BILL	Listeners may be puzzled by a taxi sounding like bagpipes. The truth is — it is all part of the BBC new economy campaign. They have discovered that it is cheaper to travel by bagpipes — not only are they more musical, but they come in a wide variety of colours. See your local Bagpipe Offices and ask for particulars — you won't be disappointed.
SPIKE	It's all rather confusing, really . . .

PETER	Meantime, Neddie Seagoon had arrived at the Bexhill Gas and Coke Works.
SEAGOON	Phewwwwwww blimeyyyyy — anyone about?
ODIUM	Yerererererere.
SEAGOON	Good.
ODIUM	Yerrer.
SEAGOON	I'd like a list of people who haven't paid their gas bills.
ODIUM	Yererererere —
SEAGOON	Oh, thank you. Now here's a good list — I'll try this number.
F.X.	**DIALLING.**
SEAGOON	Think we've got him this time — hello?
PETER	(Winston Churchill — distort) Ten Downing Street here.
SEAGOON	(gulp) I'm sorry.
F.X.	**CLICK.**

SEAGOON	No, it *couldn't* be him — who would *he* want to throw a Batter Pudding at?
F.X.	QUICK 'PHONE RING.
SEAGOON	Hello? Police here.
SPIKE	This is Mr Attlee — someone's just thrown a Batter Pudding at me.
ORCHESTRA	TYMPANY ROLL HELD UNDER NEXT SPEECH:—
SEAGOON	Months went by — still no sign of the Dreaded Hurler. Finally I walked the streets of Bexhill at night disguised as a human man — then suddenly!!
ORCHESTRA	FLARING CHORD.
SEAGOON	Nothing happened. But it happened suddenly. Disappointed, I lit my pipe.
F.X.	MATCH. WHOOSH OF SHELL. EXPLOSION OF SHELL.
SEAGOON	Curse those Germans.
MORIARTY	Pardon me, my friend.
SEAGOON	I turned to see the speaker — he was a tall man wearing sensible feet and a head to match. He was dressed in the full white outfit of a Savoy chef — around his waist were tied several thousand cooking instruments — behind him he pulled a portable gas stove from which issued forth the smell of Batter Pudding..
MORIARTY	Could I borrow a match? You see, my gas has gone out and my Batter Pudding was just browning.
SEAGOON	Certainly. Here — no — keep the whole box — I have another match at home.
MORIARTY	So rich. Well, thank you, m'sieu — you have saved my Batter Pudding from getting cold. There's nothing worse than being struck down with a cold Batter Pudding.
SEAGOON	Oh yes.
MORIARTY	Good night.
SEAGOON	I watched the strange man as he pulled his gas stove away into the darkness. But I couldn't waste time watching him — my job was to find the Dreaded Batter Pudding Hurler.
BILL	Those listeners who think that Seagoon is not cut out to be a detective — please write to him care of Rowton House.
SEAGOON	On December 25th the Hurler changed his tactics — that day Miss Bannister was struck with a Christmas Pudding. Naturally, I searched the workhouse.
WILLIUM	No sir — we ain't had no Christmas puddin' here, have we mate?
SPIKE	No.
WILLIUM	We ain't had none for three years, have we mate?
SPIKE	No — it's all rather annoying, really.

CRUN	*(approaching)* Ahh Mr Sniklecrum . . .
MINNIE	Ahhhhhh.
SEAGOON	Mr Crun, Miss Bannister, what are you doing here?
CRUN	Mnk, Minnie had a letter this morning.
MINNIE	I had a letter.
CRUN	Mn gnup . . . I'll tell him, Minnie.
MINNIE	Thank you, Henry.
CRUN	Mnk — yes, she had a —
MINNIE	Yess, you tell him.
CRUN	Alright, I'll tell . . .
MINNIE	. . . Yes . . .
CRUN	She had a lett . . .
SEAGOON	Yes, I know she had a letter — what about it?
CRUN	It proves that the Batter Pudding Hurler is abroad.
SEAGOON	What? Why? How?
CRUN	It was post-marked Africa — and inside was a portion of Batter Puddin'.
MINNIE	Yes — he hasn't forgotten me.
SEAGOON	So he's in Africa — now we've got him cornered. I must leave at once. Bluebottle!
BLUEBOTTLE	I heard you call, my Capatain — I heard my Captain call — waits for audience applause — not a sausage — puts on I don't care expression as done by Aneurin Bevan at Blackpool Conservative Rally.
SEAGOON	Bluebottle — you and I are going to Africa.
BLUEBOTTLE	Good — can we take sandwiches?
SEAGOON	Only for food — any questions?
BLUEBOTTLE	No.
SEAGOON	I can't answer that — can you?
BLUEBOTTLE	No.
SEAGOON	Ignorant swine. Got that down, Sergeant Throat?
THROAT	Yes.
SEAGOON	Good.
THROAT	Yes.
SEAGOON	Right, we catch the very next troop convoy to Algiers. And who better to drive us out of the country than Ray Ellington and his Quartet?

QUARTET	'OL' MAN RIVER'.
	(Applause)
ORCHESTRA	'VICTORY AT SEA' THEME.
PETER	And now ...
F.X.	WASH OF WAVES ON SHIP'S PROW.
BILL	Seagoon and Bluebottle travelled by sea. To avoid detection by enemy U-boats they spoke German throughout the voyage, heavily disguised as Spaniards.
PETER	As an added precaution they travelled on separate decks and wore separate shoes on different occasions.
SEAGOON	The ship was disguised as a train — to make the train sea-worthy it was done up to look like a boat and painted to appear like a tram.
SPIKE	... All rather confusing, really.
SEAGOON	Also on board were Major Bloodnok and his regiment. When we were ten miles from Algiers we heard a dreaded cry.
ECCLES	*(off)* Mine ahead — dreadful sea-mine ahead.
BLOODNOK	*(approach)* What's happening here — why are all these men cowering down on deck, the cowards?
SEAGOON	There's a mine ahead.
BLOODNOK	Mi —
F.X.	HURRIED FOOTSTEPS AWAY AND THEN SPLASH.

SEAGOON	Funny — he wasn't dressed for swimming.
ECCLES	Hey, dere's no need to worry about the mine.
BLUEBOTTLE	Yes, I must worry — I don't want to be deaded — I'm wearing my best sports shirt. (Hurriedly puts on cardboard tin hat.)
ECCLES	Don't worry — dat mine, it can't hurt us — it's one of ours.
F.X.	EXPLOSION.
SEAGOON	Eccles, is the ship sinking?
ECCLES	Only below the sea.
SEAGOON	We must try and save the ship — help me get it into the lifeboat.
ECCLES	O.K. . . . . Upppppppppp.
BOTH	(Grunts and groans)

ECCLES	It's no good, the ship won't fit in the lifeboat.
SEAGOON	What a ghastly oversight by the designer. Never mind, it leaves room for one more in the boat.
BLOODNOK	I'm willing to fill that vacancy.
SEAGOON	How did you get back on board?
BLOODNOK	I was molested by a lobster with a disgusting mind.
SEAGOON	Right, Bloodnok, do your duty.
BLOODNOK	(calls) Women and children first.
SEAGOON	Bloodnok, take that dummy out of your mouth.
ECCLES	Hey, don't leave me behind.
BLOODNOK	And why not?
ECCLES	. . . Give me time and I'll think of a reason.

BLOODNOK	Right, wait here until Apple Blossom Time — meantime, Seagoon, lower away.
F.X.	WINCHES GOING.
ECCLES	Hey — if you make room for me, I'll pay ten pounds.
F.X.	SPLASH.
SEAGOON	*(off)* You swine Bloodnok —
BLOODNOK	Business is business — get in, Eccles
ECCLES	Ta.
SEAGOON	*(off)* Look, I'll pay *twenty* pounds for a place in the boat.
F.X.	SPLASH.
BLOODNOK	*(off)* Aeiough, you double-crosser, Eccles.
ECCLES	Get in, Captain Seagoon.
HARRY	Ahhh, thank you Eccles — myyy friend.
BLOODNOK	*(off)* Thirty pounds for a place.
F.X.	SPLASH.
ECCLES	*(off)* *You ain't* my friend.
BLOODNOK	Ahhhh, good old Seagoon, you've saved me.
SEAGOON	My pal.
ECCLES	*(off)* Fifty pounds for a place in the boat.
F.X.	TWO DISTANT SPLASHES.
SPIKE	Alert listeners will have heard two splashes — this means that both Bloodnok *and* Seagoon have been hurled in the water — *who* could have done this?
BLUEBOTTLE	Ha heuheuheuheuheuhuh — I dood it I doo — I hid behind a tin of dry biscuits and then I grabbed their tootsies and upppp into the water — ha heheu huehhhhh —
ECCLES	Bluebottle, you saved my life.
BLUEBOTTLE	O ha well, we all make mistakes! I like this game — what school do you go to?
ECCLES	Reform. *(Both fading off)*

SEAGOON	Tricked by the brilliant planning of Bluebottle and Eccles, Bloodnok and I floundered in the cruel sea.
F.X.	SEA.
BLOODNOK	Fortunately we found a passing lifeboat and dragged ourselves aboard.
SEAGOON	We had no oars but luckily we found two outboard motors and we rowed with them.
BLOODNOK	Brilliant.
SEAGOON	For thirty days we drifted to and fro — then hunger came upon us.
BLOODNOK	Aeioughhhhhhhh — if I don't eat soon I'll die and if I die I won't eat soon. Wait — *(sniffffff)* can I smell cooking or do my ears deceive me?
SEAGOON	He was right — he has smelly ears — something was cooking — there in the other end of the lifeboat was — a gas stove! Could this be the end of our search?
BLOODNOK	I'll knock on the oven door.
F.X.	KNOCKING ON OVEN DOOR.
MORIARTY	*(off)* Just a minute, I'm in the bath . . . *(Pause)*
F.X.	COMING DOWN IRON STAIRS. MORIARTY SINGING. OVEN DOOR OPENS.
MORIARTY	Good morning — I'm sorry — *you*!!!
SEAGOON	Yes — remember Bexhill — I lent you the matches.
MORIARTY	You don't want them back?
SEAGOON	Don't move — I arrest you as the Dreaded Batter Pudding Hurler. Hands up, you devil — don't move — this finger is loaded.
MORIARTY	If you kill me I promise you'll never take me alive.
BLOODNOK	Wait — how can we prove it?
SEAGOON	That Batter Pudding in the corner of the stove is all the evidence we need. We've got him.
ORCHESTRA	CRASHING TRIUMPHANT THEME.
F.X.	QUIET SEA. LAPPING OF WAVES.
BILL	But it wasn't easy — forty days they drifted in an open boat.
FIDDLE	'HEARTS AND FLOWERS'.
BLOODNOK	Oooaeioughhh, I tell you Seagoon — let's eat the Batter Pudding or we'll starve!!
SEAGOON	No, d'yer hear me — no! That's the only evidence we've got — though I must admit this hunger does give one an appetite.
BLOODNOK	We must eat it or die.
SEAGOON	Never!!!

BLOODNOK	We must.
BOTH	*(Fade off)*
BILL	And that, we fear, is the end of our story except, of course, for the end — we invite listeners to submit what they think should be the classic ending. Should Seagoon eat the Batter Pudding and live or leave it and in the cause of justice — die? Meantime, for those of you cretins who would like a happy ending — here it is.
GRAMS	SWEET BACKGROUND MUSIC, VERY, VERY SOFT.
HARRY	Darling — darling, will you marry me?
BLOODNOK	Of course I will — darling.
BILL	Thank you — good night.
ORCHESTRA	SIGNATURE TUNE: UP AND DOWN FOR:—
BILL	That was The Goon Show — a recorded programme featuring Peter Sellers, Harry Secombe and Spike Milligan with the Ray Ellington Quartet and Max Geldray. The Orchestra was conducted by Wally Stott. Script by Spike Milligan. Announcer: Wallace Greenslade. The programme produced by Peter Eton.
ORCHESTRA	SIGNATURE TUNE UP TO END.
	(Applause)
MAX & ORCHESTRA	'CRAZY RHYTHM' PLAYOUT.

THE PHANTOM HEAD·SHAVER

(OF BRIGHTON)

The Goon Show: No. 103 (5th Series, No. 4)
Transmission: Tuesday, 15th October 1954:
8.30—9.00 p.m. Home Service
Studio: Paris Cinema, London

The main characters

Mrs Prunella Dirt	Peter Sellers
Mr Nugent Dirt	Harry Secombe
Moriarty	Spike Milligan
Usher	Ray Ellington
Judge Schnorrer	Peter Sellers
Windermere Ropesock, Q.C.	Spike Milligan
Willium (the window cleaner)	Peter Sellers
Hairy Seagoon, Q.C.	Harry Secombe
Throat	Spike Milligan
Mr Henry Crun	Peter Sellers
Miss Minnie Bannister	Spike Milligan
Bluebottle	Peter Sellers
Eccles	Spike Milligan
Major Denis Bloodnok	Peter Sellers

The Ray Ellington Quartet
Max Geldray
Orchestra Conducted by Wally Stott
Announcer: Wallace Greenslade
Script by Spike Milligan
Production by Peter Eton

During the hot summer of 1898 Mr and Mrs Nugent Dirt were just one of many honeymoon couples enjoying the bracing air of Brighton. Then, one torrid night, like a bolt from the blue the Phantom Head Shaver struck, and Mr Dirt woke up – bald! Prunella, his wife, summoned him for concealing his baldness during courtship, and the great Q.C., Hairy Seagoon, was briefed for the defence. No sooner had he arrived on the scene than the dreaded Phantom struck again! This time the victim was Mr Seagoon. As the court case dragged on, the Head Shaver struck again and again – fifty times – until Brighton became a city of terror. The Military flung a cordon round the district, leaving only one exit at Haywards Heath, and it was there, in a lonely railwayman's hut, that the fearless Hairy Seagoon finally came to grips with the dreaded 'Shaver'...

BILL	This is the BBC Home Service.
F.X.	PENNY IN MUG.
BILL	Thank you. Tonight's broadcast comes to you from an Arab Stench-Recuperating Centre in Stoke Poges. The play is considered unsuitable for people.
HARRY	Mr. Greenslade refers, of course, to the highly esteemed Goon Show.
ORCHESTRA	'WHO WERE YOU WITH LAST NIGHT' VERY FAST. RAZZ MA TAZZ.
HARRY	Ah, what a composer that Fred Wagner was. Now, tonight, the Goons — with the aid of a calibrated Turkish boot lathe and a portable volcano net — will re-enact a drama of crime. Mr. Greenslade?
BILL	Yes, sir?
HARRY	Tell the eager masses what we have in store for them.
BILL	Rubbish.
HARRY	Thank you. Yes, it's rubbish — but to make it more interesting we call it —
F.X.	RAZOR STROPPING (VALET AUTO STROP).
PETER	'The Phantom Head Shaver of Brighton'.
ORCHESTRA	DRAMATIC THEME
SPIKE	(vicar) It started in Brighton — 1898 — the year of the great Edison Bell.
HARRY	Yes — I often heard it ringing in the night.
F.X.	BIG BEN PLAYED VERY FAST MIXED WITH ANY ODD SOUNDS THAT GO WITH IT.
HARRY	Midnight o'clock and a half quarter — six and seven-eighths or thereabouts! Sleeping peacefully in the Hotel Fred are the delightful young newlyweds Nugent and Mrs. Dirt.
SPIKE	(vicar) Suddenly! In their room —
MRS DIRT	(old gal) OooooooOO! HelPPPPPPPPPPPP! HELPPPPPPPPPP! Oh! Look at his bonce! Ohhh!
NUGENT DIRT	(Bogg) Prunella, are you awake, dearest heart?
MRS DIRT	Get away from me with that dirty big bald head.
NUGENT DIRT	Bald head?
BOTH	(Panic)
F.X.	DOOR BURSTS OPEN.
MORIARTY	(approach) Please, please, Madame, M'sieu — all this noise — you are waking up all the other honeymoon couples — now what is the trouble?
MRS DIRT	It's 'im — my husband — look at him.
MORIARTY	He appears to be a perfectly normal freak.

NUGENT DIRT	If I get off this billiard table I'll strike you down —
MRS DIRT	You shut up — baldy.
NUGENT DIRT	What's all this baldy stuff — I'm not bald.
MORIARTY	The madame is right — you are — bald!
ORCHESTRA	**CRASHING THEME.**

BILL	Poor Nugent Dirt — indeed he was hairless. The Phantom Head Shaver had struck. The day after, I, Wallace Greenslade, opened a little tobacco kiosk. It was that week that Nugent Dirt was taken to court by his wife.
OMNES	*(Courtroom murmurs)*
F.X.	**THREE LOUD GAVEL BANGS.**
USHER	Silence in court — silence! The court will now stand for Judge Schnorrer — and if you'll stand for him you'll stand for anything.
JUDGE SCHNORRER	*(schmoolick)* Rite — get seated, let the mularky start.
USHER	M'lud — first case — Mrs. Dirt versus Mr. Dirt. Mrs. Prunella Dirt?
MRS DIRT	Yes, mate?
USHER	Raise yer right hand and yer left leg. Now, do you swear to tell the truth, the whole truth, and nothing but the truth?
MRS DIRT	I do.
USHER	*(sotto)* Well, *you* ain't gonna get far. M'lud — the witness for the persecution is ready.
JUDGE SCHNORRER	Rite — let the prosecuting council start his spiel.

ROPESOCK	M'lud — my client, Mrs. Prunella Dirt, claims that her husband, Nugent Dirt, did deceive her in that during their courting days, right up to their marriage night, he did in fact conceal his baldness from her without her knowledge. She discovered this sad state when, at one o'clock in the morning of the honeymoon night, she —
JUDGE SCHNORRER	(*drooling*) Go on — go on — go on —
ROPESOCK	M'lud, please — at one o'clock in the morning, Madame Dirt arose to clean the windows.

WILLIUM	I object.
ROPESOCK	Who are you?
WILLIUM	I'm the window cleaner.
ROPESOCK	I don't wish to know that. The fact that she was cleaning the windows is unimportant.
WILLIUM	My bread and butter.
ROPESOCK	What about your bread and butter?
WILLIUM	I clean the windows with it.
USHER	Silence in court!
SEAGOON	M'lud, as council for the defence, I think we are straying from the facts. My client is accused of hiding a bald head. He denies this emphatically. He claims he was shaved in the night with a razor — by person or persons unknown.
OMNES	(*Buzz of excitement . . . gets out of hand*)
JUDGE SCHNORRER	Silence in court!
SEAGOON	Silence in court!

JUDGE SCHNORRER	Silence!
SEAGOON	Silence!
JUDGE SCHNORRER	Silence!
SEAGOON	Yes, silence!
JUDGE SCHNORRER	Thank you. Now, I want to —
USHER	Silence in court!
JUDGE SCHNORRER	Silence!
SEAGOON	Silenceee!
JUDGE SCHNORRER	Silenceee there!
USHER	Silence in court!
F.X.	GAVEL BANGING STARTS AND CONTINUES:—
JUDGE SCHNORRER	Silenceeeeeeeee!
USHER	Silenceeeeeee!
OMNES & ORCHESTRA	(*Uproar*)
GRAMS	MIX IN BATTLE SCENE.
BILL	Yes, I remember the case because during the recess I did a brisk trade in my little tobacco kiosk — one of my *best* clients was the defending council, Q.C. Hairy Seagoon.
SEAGOON	(*coughs*) Yes, I smoked heavily during the trial. It was one evening as I puffed on my alabaster meersham pipe that events took a turn in the favour of Nugent Dirt.
F.X.	KNOCK ON DOOR. DOOR OPENS.
SEAGOON	Oh, a parcel!
THROAT	Yes.
SEAGOON	For me?
THROAT	Yes.
F.X.	PAPER PARCEL BEING OPENED.
SEAGOON	I wonder what it can be? Good heavens — is it? Yes — it's hair — human hair — and a note — 'Nugent Dirt is innocent — this hair is his — it was I who balded him while he slept — Signed — *The Phantom Head Shaver*'!
ORCHESTRA	THREE MORE CONCLUSIVE CHORDS.
USHER	The case of Dirt versus Dirt — third week.
JUDGE SCHNORRER	Now, then, Nugent Dirt — the jury of three just men and twenty-nine criminals finds you guilty of hiding your bald nut from your wife until after you had married her.
NUGENT DIRT	(*Bogg*) It's a lie.

JUDGE SCHNORRER	Silence!
NUGENT DIRT	(*Bogg*) Silence!
JUDGE SCHNORRER	Thank you. Therefore — I sentence you to pay a fine of three shillings or do sixty years in the nick.
NUGENT DIRT	I'll do the sixty years — I'm not throwing three bob down the drain.
JUDGE SCHNORRER	Dirt — for refusing to throw three bob down the drain I sentence you to sixty years in the nick. Any last request?
NUGENT DIRT	Yes. — I want to hear 'I can't believe that you're in love with me'. Thank you.
JUDGE SCHNORRER	Call Max Geldray.
MAX & ORCHESTRA	MUSIC.
	(*Applause*)
JUDGE SCHNORRER	Silence, silence in court! What a load of rough we get here . . .
SEAGOON	(*triumphant*) M'lud — stop the case! Stop the case! I have here evidence that will *prove* my client Nugent Dirt innocent! See — this hair is his — I submit it for analysis.
JUDGE SCHNORRER	Ohh, my life! Have we got to go through all this again? Orl rite — case suspended until the hair is analysed, and proved to be or not to be Nugent Dirt's.
OMNES	(*Murmurs*)

ORCHESTRA	HARP.
BILL	The days of waiting for the analysis of the hair were agony for Hairy Seagoon — he smoked pipe after pipe of one of my special tobaccos.
SEAGOON	(*coughing*) Gad, this tobacco! (*Cough*) I *must* tell Mr. Greenslade not to make it so strong.
F.X.	KNOCK ON DOOR. DOOR OPENS.

SEAGOON	Oh — another parcel?
THROAT	Yes.
SEAGOON	Any message?
THROAT	No.
SEAGOON	Good night.
THROAT	Good night.
F.X.	DOOR CLOSES.
SEAGOON	See what's in this one . . .
F.X.	PAPER OPENING.
SEAGOON	Empty! Wait, here's a note. 'Dear Seagoon — I struck again last night — this time I have not sent you the victim's hair — Signed — *The Phantom Head Shaver.*' Mmm 'P.S. If you want to know who the victim is — look in the mirror.' *(Pause)* Ahhhhhhhhh — I've been balded — he's balded me — ohhhhhhhhh!
ORCHESTRA	THREE SINISTER CHORDS. SOFT AND LOW.

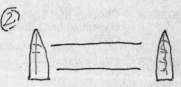

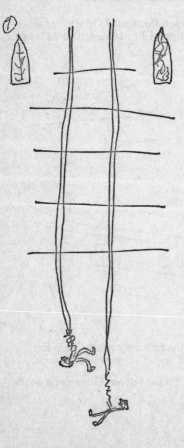

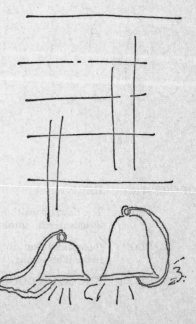

BILL	Poor Seagoon — all his lovely hair gone. The following day I opened up a *larger* shop as my supplies of pipe tobacco were growing.
PETER	In the months that followed — the Phantom struck again and again! Fifty men were balded while they slept.
SPIKE	Brighton became a city of terror — the holiday trade was threatened — that year only two men came to Brighton — a hurried meeting was called.
OMNES	(*Fast murmurs*)
HARRY	(*old man*) Gentlemen — people aren't coming to Brighton — they're frightened. I ask you to think of an idea that will revive the holiday trade — and defeat the Phantom Head Shaver!
CRUN	Mnk — I suggest that every one entering Brighton be handed a bald wig and that he should sleep in that self-same wig.
MINNIE	Rubbish — if all the men wear bald wigs, the Phantom will attack the women.
CRUN	Mnk — I fear that the ladies, too, will have to wear bald wigs.
MINNIE	Rubbish — why should I wear a bald wig — I'm already bald.
CRUN	Well, wear a bald wig — mnk — with hair on.
MINNIE	Rubbish — you can't have a bald wig with hair on.
CRUN	Gnk — mnk. Why not — eh — why not?
MINNIE	Well, if a bald wig had hair on — it wouldn't be bald.
CRUN	What? What?
MINNIE	Who ever heard of a bald-headed man with hair on, eh?
CRUN	Well, I have —
MINNIE	Who? Eh? Go on, tell me, who?
CRUN	Mnk . . . no — I'm not going to tell you.
MINNIE	That's because you don't know anybody with a hairy bald head.
CRUN	Yes I do, Minnie.
MINNIE	No you don't.
CRUN	. . . yes I do.
MINNIE	Who, who? Go on, tell me who?
CRUN	I don't see why I should.
CRUN & MINNIE	(*Argue*)
	(*Pause*)
	(*Argue — drivel out*)
MINNIE	. . . because you don't know an — you don't know any one with a hairy bald head.

CRUN	(*mumbles grudgingly*) Mnk . . . I do . . . I do know somebody with a hairy bald head.
MINNIE	. . . you don't.
CRUN	Mnk — grnp — knp . . . I do.
MINNIE	Don't.
CRUN	. . . . . mnk do.
MINNIE	. . . . y'don't.
CRUN	(*heart attack*) Mnk Grmp Nuk Knup . . . I . . . Mnk. I doooooooooo.
MINNIE	You donttttttttttt.
F.X.	**CLASH OF SABRES TO MIX WITH ARGUMENT.**
CRUN & MINNIE	(*Continue normal voiced argument throughout*)
F.X.	**TWO PISTOL SHOTS — SABRES CONTINUE — ONE PISTOL SHOT.**
	(*Silence*)
CRUN	. . . . Mnk, I do.
MINNIE	. . . . don't. Anyhow I'm going home — and I say you don't know a bald man with hair on his head, so <u>there</u>.
F.X.	**DOOR SLAMS.**
CRUN	Pah . . . . I do. I —
F.X.	**PHONE RINGS. RECEIVER.**
MINNIE	(*distort*) You don't.
CRUN	I do.
F.X.	**RECEIVER SLAMMED DOWN.**
CRUN	I do.
F.X.	**DOOR OPENS.**
MINNIE	You don't.
F.X.	**DOOR SLAMS.**
CRUN	I do, I —
F.X.	**PHONE RINGS — RECEIVER GRABBED OFF HOOK.**
CRUN	I do I do I do I do I do I do I do I do I do know a man with a hairy bald head — I do I do I do I do I do — I do, so there — I do. I do I do I do know a man with a hairy bald head . . . so there . . . I do . . .
SPIKE	Thank you. Now, could I speak to Mr. Seagoon? Hurray!
CRUN	Oh — I thought you were somebody else.
SPIKE	I am.

CRUN	For you.
SEAGOON	Hello, Seagoon here.
F.X.	PENNY IN MUG.
SEAGOON	Thank you.
SPIKE	Just a moment — you're through.
PETER	(*Sanders*) Hello, Seagoon?
SEAGOON	Yes.
PETER	Forensic Laboratory here.
SEAGOON	Oh, I'm pleased to meet you — you must excuse my appearance.
PETER	That hair we analysed —
SEAGOON	Yes yes yes yes yes yes yes yes yes?
PETER	. . . . please don't do that.
SEAGOON	The hair, what about the hair?
PETER	It wasn't hair — it was tobacco.
SEAGOON	What? In that case — Ellington, play while I mediatate. Exit left, smoking.
QUARTET	MUSIC.
	(*Applause*)

PETER	The Phantom Head Shaver of Brighton, Part Three.
SEAGOON	By now the position was serious. All told, three hundred men had been balded by the Phantom.
BILL	My tobacco stocks were now quite high.
SPIKE	The Military authorities had ringed the town with troops.
PETER	The only exit — Haywards Heath —
SEAGOON	(*coughs*) I'll go and seek this Phantom myself — Bluebottle?
BLUEBOTTLE	I heard you call, my Capatain — I heard my little ragged capatain call — enter Bluebottle — pauses for audience applause — not a sausage — strikes defiant Alan Ladd pose but trousers fall down and ruin effect.

SEAGOON	Little brave lad — tonight we ride to Haywards Heath to track down the Phantom Head Shaver. Are you ready?
BLUEBOTTLE	I am ready, my Capatain — let justice be doned. He will fall under the wrath of my *Boys' Wonder* mag cardboard sword. (Pulls up trousers — tucks in shirt.) Hehuehuehueu — my hands are cold.
SEAGOON	The Shaver's a dangerous man — he might kill.
BLUEBOTTLE	(*gulp*) . . . . he he he he he he — I just remembered — it's my turn to clean out the rabbit hutch.
SEAGOON	Come here, Bluebottle — don't tell me you're a coward?
BLUEBOTTLE	All right, I won't. But you're bound to hear about it sometime.
SEAGOON	Come, little spotted dick — to Haywards Heath!
BLUEBOTTLE	Ride, vaquero, ride. Olé!!
ORCHESTRA	DICK BARTON GALLOP. WITH:—
F.X.	HORSES' HOOVES.
BILL	To Haywards Heath they rode — to the exit that was guarded by the best of British troops.
ECCLES	Hi dump eper dump yump dump er — ohhhhhh — I hup etc. etc. Halt, who goes dere? Anybody dere? Halt or I fire — fire or I halt — halt — anybody out dere in the dark, anybody? If dere's anybody dere, speak up — if there nobody — keep quiet. Halt, anybody dere, I can see you — ohhh de di dum deeee di dummm. Halt, who goes dere —?
BLOODNOK	Eccles? Will you get out of that bed and get outside on guard — aeiough . . . Get out or I'll tell about the Naffi funds.
ECCLES	O.K. I'm . . .
F.X.	DOOR SLAMS.
ECCLES	Ooooooo — it's dark out here — but I'm not afraid.
SEAGOON	I say —
F.X.	DOOR OPENS AND SHUTS.
ECCLES	Who's dat? Halt, who goes — dere?
BLOODNOK	I warn you, sir — come one step nearer and we'll scream.
SEAGOON	Have no fear, I'm Q.C. Hairy Seagoon — defending council in the Nugent Dirt case. I have on me several documents of identification — including a letter of personal trust from the Commander of the British Army; a memo of recommendation from Mr. Anthony Eden, the Foreign Secretary; a special pass signed by Mr. Clement Atlee, Leader of the Opposition; and last but not least, a permit to go where I please, signed by the Prime Minister the Right Honourable Sir Winston Spencer Churchill.
ECCLES	Friend or foe?
SEAGOON	Open the door!
F.X.	DOOR OPENS.

BLOODNOK	I surrender — Pax — I'm unarmed — you wouldn't hit a nursing mother.
SEAGOON	Major Bloodnok — take off that Anna Neagle disguise. My ADC Bluebottle and I have followed a trail of hair to this post — we believe the Phantom Head Shaver is in the vicinity.
ECCLES	Well, wait till he comes out!
BLOODNOK	I tell you, sir, the Phantom wouldn't *dare* come near here — not with old Bloodnok on duty. Why, I haven't slept for *three* nights — I've just sat here waiting fer him — oh, old Bloodnok needs a smart man to outwit him. If the Phantom Head Shaver were to — what are you staring at?
SEAGOON	Do you usually have half your head shaved?
BLOODNOK	What? Ohh, tunnedd, aeioughhhh — bleiough! Aeioughhhh bleioughh ohhhhhh, tunned me gronkers with a gritclub — Ohhh ohhh ooohhh ohhhh ohhh ohhh ohhhhhhh.
SEAGOON	Something in his voice told me he knew what had happened.
BLOODNOK	Ohh — look at me nut — half balded, ohhhh!
SEAGOON	There, there, Major — this is really a blessing in disguise. You see, I must have interrupted him in his work — and we all know that a criminal always returns to the scene of the crime.
BLOODNOK	What — yer mean you want me to wait here for him to come back and shave the other half?
SEAGOON	It's your duty.
BLOODNOK	I refuse.
SEAGOON	Then, under Chinese law, I subpoena you.
BLOODNOK	You filthy swine — ohh! Very well, I'll do it. Just hand me that book about the Scottish Regiments.

NIGHT RIDE

SEAGOON	But it's called The Decameron.
BLOODNOK	Of course — it's all about Decameron Highlanders — aeiough.
SEAGOON	Right, we'll leave you and . . .
F.X.	DOOR BURSTS OPEN.
BLUEBOTTLE	Captain, Capatain — I can hear someone in the ammunition hut — it sounds like a man sharpening a dirty big razor.
SEAGOON	Quick — follow me.
F.X.	WHOOSH.
SEAGOON	(out of breath) Listen —
F.X.	RAZOR BEING STROPPED.
SEAGOON	(whisper) He's in this hut with a naked razor! Eccles, surround him!
ECCLES	Ooooooooooo.
SEAGOON	(aloud) Come out, Phantom Head Shaver — you're surrounded, d'yer hear? We're all heavily armed — if you don't come out we'll come to that door — and so help me — we'll knock!
ECCLES	Yer — yer — if you don't come out we'll knock — ha —
SEAGOON	Shut up.
ECCLES	Shut up.
BLUEBOTTLE	We're not afraid of you, Phantom Nut Shaver — we have no fear. Come out and face me — come on and show your face. (Looks out from behind tree to see if he's showing his face.)
SEAGOON	Bluebottle — go in and get him.
BLUEBOTTLE	Yes — go in and get hi — me? Me go and get him, Capatain?
SEAGOON	Yes.
BLUEBOTTLE	What, little me? Go and get him?
SEAGOON	Yes.
BLUEBOTTLE	What, little tiny rotten weak frightened Bluebottle go in and get him?
SEAGOON	Yes.
BLUEBOTTLE	. . . . . I don't like this game, let's play another game — let's play doctors and nurses.
F.X.	WHOOSH.
SEAGOON	Come down from that tree.
BLUEBOTTLE	I'll be the nurse — Florence Nightingoon, the Lady with the Lump.
F.X.	WHOOSH.
SEAGOON	Come out of that dustbin.

BLUEBOTTLE	You be the doctor.
F.X.	WHOOSH.
SEAGOON	Come out from behind that rock — the Phantom won't harm you — not when he sees that you're armed with a Jet Morgan carboard cutout space catapult.
BLUEBOTTLE	Alright, Capatain, I will go in — I trust you — I shall conquer him in mortal combat. (Quickly makes out last will and testament on back of fag packet.) In I go — farewell! I go in for England.
ORCHESTRA	FANFARE OF TRUMPETS.
BLUEBOTTLE	. . . . . let's play doctors and nurses.
ECCLES	He's frightened — why don't you send somebody else?
SEAGOON	You then.
ECCLES	Try again.
SEAGOON	Bluebottle, get in that hut and search it from end to end.
BLUEBOTTLE	O.K.
F.X.	DOOR OPENS AND SLAMS.
	(Pause)
F.X.	DOOR OPENS.
BLUEBOTTLE	Not a soul was in dere — we must have been hearing things — ha ha heuh, what a relief . . . ha heuheuheuheu. What are you starin' at me for?
SEAGOON	Look in this mirror.
BLUEBOTTLE	Oooooooo, you rotten swine — I've been balded — you've ruined my Tony Curtis haircut. Ohhh, you rotten — I told you I didn't like this game.
SEAGOON	Sh! He's still in there. I'll fix him — throw this stick of dynamite in through the door.
ECCLES	O.K.
	(Pause)
F.X.	FUSE BURNING. STOPS WITH SPLUTTER.
SEAGOON	Curse, it was a dud. Let's go in — come on, keep me covered with your finger —
F.X.	DOOR OPENS — MAMMOTH EXPLOSION — SPLINTERING GLASS — BITS OF NUTS & BOLTS FALLING — FORKS, SPOONS, ETC.
BLOODNOK	(approaching) What's going on here? What's going on? I — good heavens!
BILL	The — er — hut blew up.
BLOODNOK	Oh, poor fellows! They were looking for the Head Shaver, yer know.

BILL	*Yes* — I know . . .
BLOODNOK	I suppose he was blown up as well?
BILL	(*pause*) Care for a pipe of tobacco?
BLOODNOK	What? Oh! Thank you!
BILL	Good night.
BLOODNOK	Goodnight — charming fellow. Tobacco, eh? Gad, its the same colour as my hair — yes — it *is* the same col — Stop! That man — stop!
ORCHESTRA	SIGNATURE TUNE: UP AND DOWN FOR:—
BILL	That was The Goon Show — a recorded programme featuring Peter Sellers, Harry Secombe and Spike Milligan with the Ray Ellington Quartet and Max Geldray. The Orchestra was conducted by Wally Stott. Script by Spike Milligan. Announcer: Wallace Greenslade. The programme produced by Peter Eton.
ORCHESTRA	SIGNATURE TUNE UP TO END.
	(*Applause*)
MAX & ORCHESTRA	'CRAZY RHYTHM' PLAYOUT.

THE AFFAIR OF
THE LONE BANANA

The Goon Show: No. 104 (5th Series, No. 5)
Transmission: Tuesday, 26th October 1954:
8.30—9.00 p.m. Home Service
Studio: Paris Cinema, London

The main characters

Eccles	Spike Milligan
Inspector Neddie Seagoon	Harry Secombe
Gravely Headstone	Peter Sellers
Lady Marks	Peter Sellers
Mr Henry Crun	Peter Sellers
Miss Minnie Bannister	Spike Milligan
Señor Gonzales Mess, né Moriarty	Spike Milligan
Major Denis Bloodnok	Peter Sellers
Bluebottle	Peter Sellers
Cyril Cringinknutt	Peter Sellers
Fred Nurke	Peter Sellers

The Ray Ellington Quartet
Max Geldray
Orchestra Conducted by Wally Stott
Announcer: Wallace Greenslade
Script by Spike Milligan
Production by Peter Eton

Fred Nurke is missing! An over-ripe banana in a deserted Cannon Street shipping office is the only clue to his whereabouts. Inspector Ned Seagoon follows the trail to a British Embassy in South America, where he is just in time to help the Embassy staff in a brush with the rebels. Why are Señor Gonzales Mess and his gang trying to cut down the only banana tree in the Embassy gardens? And what is the connection between Fred Nurke and the over-ripe banana in Cannon Street? We shall see...

BILL	This is the BBC Home Service.
GRAMS	WAILING.
HARRY	Yes indeed — to the gay music of Britain's taxpayers, we present the Grune Show.
ORCHESTRA	VERY LONG VIGOROUS SYMPHONIC FINISH A LA 'WILLIAM TELL'.
F.X.	EXPLOSION — FALLING GLASS, BITS & PIECES.
SPIKE	And why not?
HARRY	Yes, why not? Mr. Greenslade!
BILL	Yes, Master?
HARRY	Tell the masses what's the play.
BILL	Ladies and gentlemen . . .
HARRY	Thank you. Yes, it's ladies and gentlemen in . . . 'The Affair of the Lone Banana'!
ORCHESTRA	DEEP SINISTER CHORDS HELD UNDER:—
PETER	The Affair of the Lone Banana — not a pretty story, I fear; still, the BBC *will* buy this cheap trash. However . . . the central character in this story is young Fred Nurke. His father, Lord Marks, made a fortune from the great Marks Laundry business . . . but then you've all heard of Laundry Marks . . . ha ha ha. But let's start the story from the beginning.
ORCHESTRA	'GREENSLEEVES'-TYPE MUSIC . . . FLUTE, HARP TO BACKGROUND FOR:—
BILL	The scene is the country home of the Marks, Matzos Lodge. A mystery has been committed: young Fred Nurke has vanished. Interrogating the residents is a man, tall, dark, handsome, swashbuckling, handsome, intelligent . . .
ECCLES	This ain't me, folks — I come in later.
BILL	No — it's Inspector Neddie Seagoon, late of the eighteenth century and part inventor of the steam-driven explodable hairless toupée.
SEAGOON	. . . Now then my man, your name is — er?
HEADSTONE	Headstone, Gravely Headstone. My maiden name, you understand.
SEAGOON	I understand. *(Aside)* Don't put that down, Sergeant.
THROAT	Right, sir.
SEAGOON	Headstone, you are a footman.
HEADSTONE	Two foot six to be exact.
SEAGOON	How lovely to be tall. Headstone, you say Fred Nurke disappeared whilst having a bottle of tea with his mother, Lady Marks.
HEADSTONE	True — you might say he disappeared from under her very nose.

SEAGOON	What was he doing there?
HEADSTONE	It was raining, I believe.
SEAGOON	*(self)* Mmm, Lady Marks. *(Normal)* Where is her ladyship at the moment?
HEADSTONE	Me lady hasn't got a ship at the moment.
SEAGOON	I don't wish to know that. Greenslade? Send in Lady Marks or that idiot gardener — he might know something.
BILL	Right sir. *(Calls)* Right, this way you!
F.X.	**GREAT HEAVY APPROACHING FOOTSTEPS.**
SEAGOON	Ah, Lady Marks, sit down.
LADY MARKS	Thank you.
ECCLES	I bet you all thought it was going to be me. Ha hum.
SEAGOON	Lady Marks — your late husband owned a banana plantation, yes?
LADY MARKS	In South America.
SEAGOON	That's abroad, isn't it?
LADY MARKS	It all depends on where you're standing.
SEAGOON	Let's put it this way. Is it on the tube?
LADY MARKS	Silly, silly boy.
SEAGOON	Please, madam, don't be so evasive. If South America is on the tube — we have ways and means of finding out.
LADY MARKS	Dear midget, of course it's not on the tube.
SEAGOON	Now you're talking.
LADY MARKS	So are you, isn't it fun?
SEAGOON	Lady Marks — this is a tricky case — I don't think I can —
LADY MARKS	*(plead)* Inspector, you must find my son — you must — I don't care how much money you spend — in fact, I'll chip in a few bob myself.
SEAGOON	The offer is tempting. Very well, I accept. Just leave everything to me — your purse, jewels, cheque book *(fading)* war bonds, trombone . . .

GRAMS	'HARRY LIME THEME'.
PETER	*(Barton)* At the British Passport office in Whitechapel, Seagoon discovered that Fred Nurke had left for Guatemala on a banana boat — disguised as a banana.
SEAGOON	That's true — I waited for the ship to return but he wasn't on board — he must have got off — at the other side.
ORCHESTRA & OMNES	*(Loud applause . . . cries of 'Bravo' etc . . .)*
SEAGOON	Thank you, thank you — no, don't make it sound rehearsed. My next task was to book a ticket to South America. This I did at a shipping office in Leadenhall Street.
F.X.	SHOP BELL.
CRUN	Mnk — mnk grnk. Who is it? Eh eh? Who is it?
SEAGOON	Good morning.
CRUN	Thank you.
SEAGOON	I want to book to South America.
CRUN	That's abroad, sir, isn't it?
SEAGOON	Yes. *(Cocky)* It isn't on the tube you know.
CRUN	Isn't that wonderful — what will they think of next. Ohhh, do sit down, sir.
SEAGOON	Err — there aren't any chairs.
CRUN	You can stand up if you wish.
SEAGOON	Thank you.
CRUN	No extra charge. Now, let's get some details and documents — we must have documents, you know. I'll just take a few particulars. Now, let's get the details and the documents — we must have documents, you know.
SEAGOON	Of course.
CRUN	. . . must have documents. Ymnbnkhmn, now, what's all this about? Let me — oh yes. Now, name?
SEAGOON	Neddie Pugh Seagoon.
CRUN	*(writing)* N E D D I E . . . Neddie — what was next?
SEAGOON	Neddie *Pugh* Seagoon.
CRUN	*Pugh*, P H E W.
SEAGOON	No, it's pronounced Phew but it's spelt P U G H.
CRUN	Oh, ynmnk, P U G H — there — Neddie Pugh, Seagoon wasn't it?
SEAGOON	Yes . . . S E A G O O N.
CRUN	Could you spell it?

SEAGOON	Certainly — S E A G O O N.
CRUN	Seagoon . . . S E A G er — mnkk — mnkk. *(Goes to sleep)*
SEAGOON	G O O N — Seagoon.
CRUN	O O N — ahhh good, good, good — there, the full name. Now then — address?
SEAGOON	No fixed abode.
CRUN	N O . . . F I X E D . . . A B . . . A B —
SEAGOON	A B O D E.
CRUN	O D E . . . there — no fixed abode — what number?
SEAGOON	29A.
CRUN	Twenty nine . . . a . . . district?
SEAGOON	London, S.W.2.
CRUN	L O N D O N — S O U T H W E S T . . . *Two*, wasn't it?
SEAGOON	Yes, two.
CRUN	TW . . . It's no good, I'd better get a pencil and paper and write all this down. Minnie . . . . *Minnie*?? Min, Min, Min, Min, Min, *Minieeeeee!*
MINNIE	What is it, Henry?
CRUN	A pencil, please.
MINNIE	O.K. buddy.
CRUN	Minnie, this gentleman is going to South America.
MINNIE	Ohh — goodbye.
CRUN	That's where young Fred Nurke went to . . .
SEAGOON	Fred Nurke? That's Fred Nurke's name!
CRUN	Yes, he went in such a rush he left this behind.
SEAGOON	Let me see — a banana — a lone banana! So, now my task was easier — I knew that the man I was looking for was one banana short!
ORCHESTRA	*(Loud applause . . . shouts of 'Bravo' etc . . .)*
BILL	As a tribute to Seagoon's brilliant deductive powers, Max Geldray will now play a loaded sackbut from the kneeling position.
MAX & ORCHESTRA	MUSIC.

(Applause)

BILL   The Affair of the Lone Banana, Chapter Two. With the banana secreted on his person, Neddie Seagoon arrived at the Port of Guatemala where he was accorded the typical Latin welcome to an Englishman.

MORIARTY   Hands up, you pig swine.

SEAGOON   Have a care, Latin devil — I am an Englishman. Remember, this rolled umbrella has more uses than one.

MORIARTY   Oooo!

SEAGOON   Sorry. Now, what's all this about?

MORIARTY   It is the revolution — everywhere there is an armed rising.

SEAGOON   Are you all in it?

MORIARTY   Right in it — you see, the united anti-socialist neo-democratic pro-fascist communist party are fighting to overthrow the unilateral democratic united partisan bellicose pacifist cobelligerant tory labour liberal party

SEAGOON   Whose side are you on?

MORIARTY   There are no sides — we are all in this together. Now, if you don't mind — we must search you.

SEAGOON   What for?

MORIARTY   Bananas. You see, we Guatemalians are trying to overthrow the foreign-dominated banana plantations in this country. Any foreigner found with a banana on him will be shot by a firing squad and asked to leave the country.

SEAGOON	*(aside)* Curses — I must think quick. Little does he know I suspect him of foul play.
MORIARTY	Little does he know I've never played with a fowl in my life.
SEAGOON	Little does he know that he has misconstrued the meaning of the word foul. The word foul in my sentence was spelt F O U L not F O W L as he thought I had spelt it.
MORIARTY	Little does he know that I overheard his correction of my grammatical error and I am now about to rectify it — aloud. *(Ahem)* So, you suspect me of foul play spelt F O U L and not F O W L.
SEAGOON	Yes — and you might as well know I'm here to find young Fred Nurke.
MORIARTY	*That* capitalistic pig! Why, I'll —
SEAGOON	Don't move, Signor Gonzales Mess, né Moriarty — hands up.
MORIARTY	Seagoon, put that banana down!
SEAGOON	And leave myself defenceless?
MORIARTY	Sapristi Bompet!
SEAGOON	One step nearer and I fire.
MORIARTY	Fool — you can't shoot a banana! It's —
F.X.	TWO PISTOL SHOTS.
MORIARTY	Swine — it was *loaded*!
SEAGOON	Of course — you don't think I'd threaten you with an unloaded banana? Now come on, tell me — where is Fred Nurke?
MORIARTY	I will never tell — go on, torture me — smash my skull in — break my bones — put lighted matches in my fingers — tear the flesh from my body, slice lumps off my . . .
F.X.	THUD OF BODY FALLING ON GROUND.
MORIARTY	Pancho?
PETER	Signor?
MORIARTY	The smelling salts — he's fainted.
ORCHESTRA	THEME SPANISH. LIKE DEATH THEME FROM 'CARMEN,'. SOFTLY ON TROMBONES WITH TYMPS.
PETER	When the Englishman awoke he found himself in a tall dark room with sideboards — it was a prison cell.
SEAGOON	True, true. The only other occupant was another occupant — apart from that, he was the *only* other occupant. He was chained to the wall by a chain which was attached to the wall — he *appeared* to be a man of breeding and intellect.
ECCLES	Hello dere.
SEAGOON	J was wrong. (But wait — could he be Fred Nurke?)

ECCLES	How's yer old dad, eh?
SEAGOON	Do you recognise this banana?
ECCLES	Nope — I don't think I've ever met him before.
SEAGOON	Then — then are you one banana short?
ECCLES	Umm, nope — nope, I ain't one short.
SEAGOON	Curse — then you're *not* Fred Nurke.
ECCLES	Ohh, ain't I?
SEAGOON	No.
ECCLES	Yer mean I'm somebody else?
SEAGOON	Yes.
ECCLES	Ooo — who am I?
SEAGOON	What's your name?
ECCLES	Eccles.
SEAGOON	*That's* who you are!
ECCLES	Oooooooo.
SEAGOON	There, there, don't take it so hard. Now then, how can I get out of this place?
ECCLES	Well, there's dat door dere.
SEAGOON	Right, I'm away! By dawn I'll be safe! Now's the time for *action!* Nothing will stop me now — Farewellllllll!
F.X.	DOOR OPENS AND CLOSES. TERRIFIC FUSILLADE OF SHOTS, BOMBS, ETC. DOOR OPENS AND CLOSES.
SEAGOON	It's raining! Is there any other way out of here?

ECCLES	Would you care to share my supper?
SEAGOON	Ahh, how about that window up there!
ECCLES	Oh, you can't eat that.
SEAGOON	If we could get up to that window.
ECCLES	Well, get dis iron chain off my neck and I'll help.
SEAGOON	Right — just put your neck on this block — I'll soon have it off.
F.X.	IRON HAMMER ON ANVIL. THREE HEFTY WHACKS. CHAINS FALL TO FLOOR.
SEAGOON	There — that's broken it — you're free! How do you feel?
ECCLES	Don't know — ain't ever had a broken neck before.
SEAGOON	Come, let's to the task!
ECCLES	O.K.
F.X.	CHAIRS BEING STACKED ONE ON TOP OF THE OTHER. THIS NOISE KEPT GOING IN BACKGROUND.
BILL	Ladies and gentlemen, the sound you are hearing is that of Seagoon and Eccles balancing chairs one atop the other. This operation might last some time as they will need to stack at least fifty to a hundred chairs if they are to reach up to the high window. No doubt, after about five minutes, this sound will become very boring — BBC policy therefore decrees that in the interim we entertain you with songs from that well known tenor and market gardener — Mr. Cyril Cringinknutt.
CRINGINKNUTT	(Izzy) Thankin' yew — Rinky Fulton. My first number tonight I will sing for money — that lovely Yock melody from my latest record which I have just recorded. It's called 'Three Goons in a Fountain' — my melody please, Fred —
PIANO	ARPEGGIO.
CRINGINKNUTT	(croon) Three Goons in a fountain — which one will the fountain drown — I got a shop full of Schmutters — I got —
BILL	Thank you. Ladies and gentlemen — Seagoon and Eccles have reached the high window so we won't need Cyril Cringinknutt any more, so we'll say—
F.X.	ALL THE CHAIRS COLLAPSE — TERRIFIC CRASH. START STACKING THEM UP AGAIN.
CRINGINKNUTT	Three Goons in a fountain, which one will the foun —
F.X.	DOOR BURSTS OPEN.
SPIKE	Eyes front — everyone back to their own beds. There is an English gentleman to see you.
ORCHESTRA	BLOODNOK MARCH.
BLOODNOK	Aeiough. Bleiough. Arangahahhh. Kitna Budgy Hai. Aeiough and other naughty noises. Now — which one of you two is Eccles and Seagoon?

SEAGOON	I'm Seagoon except for Eccles.
ECCLES	I'm Eccles except for Seagoon.
BLOODNOK	So, you're both Eccles and Seagoon except for each other!
SEAGOON	Yes.
BLOODNOK	I knew I'd get it out of you. I'm the British Chargé d'Affaires — Major Bloodnok, late of Zsa Zsa Gabor's Third Regular Husbands. I've managed to secure your release. I completely overcame the prison guards.
SEAGOON	What with?
BLOODNOK	Money — aeiough — now, everybody onto this ten-seater horse. Nowwww, gid up there.
F.X.	**GALLOPING HOOVES START AND STOP AT ONCE.**
BLOODNOK	Woah. Here we are. The Embassy.
F.X.	**KNOCK ON DOOR. DOOR OPENS.**
RAY	Oh, it's you, sir — am I glad you came back. The rebels have been trying to chop down the banana tree in the garden.
BLOODNOK	Dogs! Stand back. *(Shouts)* You Latin devils — begone, or by the great artificial paste earrings of Lady Barnett I'll come out there and cut you down — now get out, you Latin devils!
RAY	They all went about three hours ago.
BLOODNOK	Never mind. That didn't stop me.
SEAGOON	Gad, Bloodnok, I admire your guts.

BLOODNOK	Why, are they showing?
SEAGOON	Bloodnok, I seek Fred Nurke.
BLOODNOK	He's here to save the British banana industry. In fact, he went out alone, by himself, to dynamite the rebel H.Q.
SEAGOON	Then all we can do is wait.
BLOODNOK	Yes — Ellington? Play that mad banjo, man.
RAY	Here goes then —
QUARTET	MUSIC.

(Applause)

GRAMS	'HARRY LIME THEME'.
PETER	*(Barton)* The Affair of the Lone Banana, Chapter Three. In the grounds of the British Embassy our heroes are dug in around the lone banana tree — the last symbol of waning British prestige in South America. They all anxiously await the return of Fred Nurke. Around them, the jungle night is alive with revels — and nocturnal sounds — rain in places, fog patches on the coast. Arsenal 2 — Chinese Wanderers 600.
F.X.	BRAZILIAN JUNGLE AT NIGHT — CRICKETS — AMAZON OWLS — CHIKIKIS AND OTHER NIGHT ANIMALS.
SEAGOON	Gad, Bloodnok — this waiting is killing me.
BLOODNOK	Shhhhh — not so loud, you fool — remember, even people have ears.
SEAGOON	Sorry, Major, but my nerves are strung up to breaking point.
F.X.	ONE STRING FIDDLE. DOINGGGGG. SNAP. (QUICK)
SEAGOON	There goes one now. It's this darkness! You can't see a *thing!*
BLOODNOK	I know — for three hours now I've been straining my eyes and I've only managed *one* page of the *Awful Disclosures of Maurice Monk.* Four rupees, in a plain wrapper.

F.X.	LONE CRICKET CHIRPING.
BLOODNOK	Listen — what's making that noise?
SEAGOON	Cricket.
BLOODNOK	How can they see to bat in *this* light?
ECCLES	Major, a man's just climbed over the garden wall.
BLOODNOK	A boundary! *(Aloud)* Well played, sir!
SEAGOON	Shh, Bloodnok, you fool — that's no cricketer — he's possibly a rebel assassin.
BLOODNOK	Then one of us must volunteer to go out and get him.
SEAGOON	Yes — one of us must volunteer.
ECCLES	Yer, one of us *must* volunteer!
ALL	England for ever!
ORCHESTRA	FANFARE MILITAIRE

BILL	The Affair of the Lone Banana, Chapter Four.
BLOODNOK	One of us *must* volunteer.
SEAGOON	Yes, one of us must.
ECCLES	Yup, one of us must.
BLOODNOK	Well, who's it going to be? Seagoon?
SEAGOON	I'm sorry — but I have a wife and sixty-three children.
BLOODNOK	I too have a wife and children. That only leaves dear old —
F.X.	PANICKY RATTLING OF TELEPHONE.
ECCLES	Hello, hello, operator? Get me the marriage bureau.
BLOODNOK	Eccles, you coward. Seagoon? You're youngest, you go.
SEAGOON	Me? You wouldn't send an old man out there?
BLOODNOK	You're not an old man.
SEAGOON	Give me five minutes to make up and you'll never know the difference.
BLOODNOK	Flatten me Cronkler with Spinachmallets. So, *both* of you have turned cowards. That only leaves *me*. Two cowards, and *me*. You know what this means?
SEAGOON	*Three* cowards.
BLOODNOK	. . . in a fountain . . . Let's face it — we've all *turned yellow*.
RAY	You speak for yourselves.
BLOODNOK	*(apologetic)* Ohh, I'm sorry, Ellington, no offence. I know you Irishmen are very brave.
F.X.	PHONE RINGS.
BLOODNOK	Aeiough. Don't answer that phone unless it's for me.
SEAGOON	Right. Are you ringing for Major Bloodnok?
MORIARTY	*(distort)* Yes.
SEAGOON	It's for you.
BLOODNOK	Ohhh.
F.X.	RECEIVER OFF HOOK.
BLOODNOK	Hello? What??? Never — never, d'yer hear me? Never.
F.X.	RECEIVER SLAMMED DOWN.
BLOODNOK	It was the rebel leader — Gonzales Mess, né Moriarty, he says unless we chop down our banana tree and hand it over to them — we'll die tonight.
ECCLES	Tonight? Why, that's tonight.
BLOODNOK	So it is. Fancy him thinking *I'd* chop down the banana to save my lousy skin — ha! ha!

harry's drawing of spike →

F.X.	**HURRIED CHOPPING DOWN OF TREE.**
SEAGOON	Bloodnok! Put down that forty-ton chopper!
BLOODNOK	I'm sorry, I picked it up in a moment of weakness.
SEAGOON	Disgraceful! Chopping down the British banana tree!
ECCLES	Yer, disgraceful.
F.X.	**HURRIED SAWING OF TREE.**
SEAGOON	Eccles! Stop that! Where did you get that saw?
ECCLES	*(big joke)* From the sea — it's a sea-saw. Ha ha.
SEAGOON	Silence! We've got to pull ourselves together — this banana tree is the *last one* in South America under British control!
BLOODNOK	Yes, you're right! We must defend it, with your lives.
SEAGOON	Remember, lads — somewhere out there, Fred Nurke is working to destroy the rebel H.Q. — now, throw that chopper and saw over the wall.
BOTH	O.K. *(Grunt)*
SEAGOON	Good — now I'm —
F.X.	**CLANG AND THUD AS CHOPPER CLOUTS MAN ON NUT.**
BLUEBOTTLE	*(off)* Ohhhhh — my nut — ohh — I have been hitted on my bonce — oh, I have been nutted — I was kipping on the grass and suddenly — *thud!* Oooooh! Clutches lump on crust.
SEAGOON	Come out from behind that wall or I'll throw this at you.
ECCLES	Put me down!
BLUEBOTTLE	*(sad)* Enter Bluebottle wearing crash helmet — pauses for audience applause — not a sausage! (Thinks of rude sailor word.)
SEAGOON	Who is this gallant little knight with unlaced LCC plimsolls?
BLUEBOTTLE	Who am *I*? I'm the one wot copped that dirty big saw on the nut. (Points to lump area.)
SEAGOON	Tell me, little jam-stained hero; do you know this jungle well?
BLUEBOTTLE	Yes — I know the jungule — Tarzan Bluebottle, they call me. (Lifts up sports shirt, shows well developed ribs and bones. Fills chest with air *(breathe)* — feels giddy so puts on cardboard loin cloth for support.)
SEAGOON	Could you lead me to the rebel H.Q.?
BLUEBOTTLE	*(intimate)* I can show you the very spot.
SEAGOON	*(intimate)* Where?
BLUEBOTTLE	*(declaim)* Where that dirty big saw hitted my nut! You rotten nut-hitting swine you! (Does body racked with sobs pose — as done by Robert Newton after seeing income tax returns.)

SEAGOON	Right. Eccles, you come with us. Bloodnok — you stay here. Bluebottle — lead on!
BLUEBOTTLE	Forward! Pulls hat well down over eyes (but pulls it up as cannot see where I'm going). Come, follow me — I —
F.X.	**TERRIFYING ROAR OF SAVAGE LION.**
BLUEBOTTLE	Heu heu hu — what was that, my capatain?
SEAGOON	A man-eating tiger.
BLUEBOTTLE	Tiger?
SEAGOON	Yes.
F.X.	**WHOOSH.**
BLUEBOTTLE	*(right off)* I do not like this game — I'm going home — I just remembered it's my turn in the barrel — exits left to East Finchley on Council dust cart.
SEAGOON	Very well, I'll go ahead myself — first I'll disguise myself as a Mexican peon — they'll never recognise me!

BILL	The Affair of the Lone Banana, Chapter Five.
MORIARTY	Signor Grytpype-Thynne — we found this idiot hiding in a dustbin disguised as a Mexican peon.
GRYTPYPE-THYNNE	Ahhhh — a midget, eh?
SEAGOON	Have a care.
GRYTPYPE-THYNNE	No thanks, I don't smoke — sit on a chair.
SEAGOON	I'll stand.
GRYTPYPE-THYNNE	Very well, stand on a chair then.
SEAGOON	So — you're the leader of the rebels?
GRYTPYPE-THYNNE	Yes, now — *who are you?*

SEAGOON	*I won't talk!* Never!
GRYTPYPE-THYNNE	*(calls off)* The branding irons!
SEAGOON	I'm Neddie Seagoon.
GRYTPYPE-THYNNE	Oh? Where's Fred Nurke?
SEAGOON	I don't know.
GRYTPYPE-THYNNE	So *that's* where he is. Right, Moriarty? We'll go at once to the Embassy — and bring back their banana tree.
SEAGOON	You won't succeed — it's guarded by Major Dennis Bloodnok.
GRYTPYPE-THYNNE	Bloodnok? Moriarty — bring money. Seagoon, we'll lock you in here — goodbye.
F.X.	DOOR LOCKS — KEY.
SEAGOON	Poor fools — the moment they step out — Fred Nurke will get them — they go to their doom!
F.X.	PHONE RINGS — RECEIVER OFF HOOK.

SEAGOON	Hello?
FRED NURKE	*(distort)* Is that the rebel H.Q.?
SEAGOON	Yes, but I'm —
FRED NURKE	Right, you swines — this is Fred Nurke, and this is my bonanza night — in three seconds a time-bomb explodes in your room, ha ha!
F.X.	CLICK.
SEAGOON	Three seconds — I've got to get . . .
F.X.	FOOTSTEPS RUNNING FOR DOOR.
BILL	Will Seagoon get out in time?
F.X.	EXPLOSION.

BILL	Oh, hard luck — still, he tried. Was his sacrifice worthwhile — did Bloodnok save the banana tree?
F.X.	TREE CRACKING.
BLOODNOK	Timber!!!
F.X.	TREE CRASHING.
ORCHESTRA	SIGNATURE TUNE: UP AND DOWN FOR:—
BILL	That was The Goon Show — a recorded programme featuring Peter Sellers, Harry Secombe and Spike Milligan with the Ray Ellington Quartet and Max Geldray. The Orchestra was conducted by Wally Stott. Script by Spike Milligan. Announcer: Wallace Greenslade. The programme produced by Peter Eton.
ORCHESTRA	SIGNATURE TUNE UP TO END.
	(Applause)
MAX & ORCHESTRA	'CRAZY RHYTHM' PLAYOUT.

THE CANAL

The Goon Show: No. 105 (5th Series, No. 6)
Transmission: Tuesday, 2nd November 1954:
8.30—9.00 p.m. Home Service
Studio: Paris Cinema, London

The main characters

Ned Seagoon	Harry Secombe
Lord Valentine Seagoon	Valentine Dyall
Eccles	Spike Milligan
Flowerdew	Peter Sellers
Reuben Croucher	Peter Sellers
Major Denis Bloodnok	Peter Sellers
Gravely Headstone	Ray Ellington
Dr Justin Eidelburger	Peter Sellers
Dr Yakamoto	Spike Milligan
Mr Henry Crun	Peter Sellers
Miss Minnie Bannister	Spike Milligan
Bluebottle	Peter Sellers
Miss Throat	Spike Milligan

Special Guest: Valentine Dyall ('The Man in Black')
The Ray Ellington Quartet
Max Geldray
Orchestra Conducted by Wally Stott
Announcer: Wallace Greenslade
Script by Spike Milligan
Production by Peter Eton

After forty-three years at school, young Ned Seagoon returns to Seagoon's Folly, the ancestral home, to find it empty save for a sinister oriental valet, a refugee heroin importer and Gravely Headstone, the butler. Where is Seagoon's father, his four mothers, the first cook, the underfootman and the overfootman? All Ned's queries are met with silence. Then, one night, three mysterious strangers are seen digging a grave nearly fifty feet long in the rose-garden. Hollow knockings and weird moans are heard in the buttery and Strangler Aagonschmidt, a notorious schizophrenic, is discovered in the act of setting fire to the library. Why is there a secret passage from the grave to Seagoon's bedroom? What is the secret of 'The Canal'?

Most of the action takes place in a walled-up tomb in the crypt of Seagoon's Folly. Mysterious knockings recorded by permission of the Poltergeist Society of Lower Regent Street...

Hows yer old dad!

"ECCLES"

BILL	This is the BBC Home Service.
PETER	*(Flowerdew)* This is madness, d'you hear me? Madness!
HARRY	The man is, of course, referring to the highly esteemed Goon Show.
GRAMS	1922 JACK PAYNE RECORD OF ONE-STEP.
HARRY	Stop. Thank you, Geraldo. Mr. Greenslade, tell the eager multitudes of the goodies we have in store for them.
BILL	Ladies and Gintlepong. In keeping with the policy of our more 'popular' Sunday newspapers, we give you now a nice soggy mess of vice, drunkeness and worst of all — the shame of our cities!
PETER	*(Winston Churchill)* Mixed fretwork classes.
HARRY	Thank you, Geraldo. To commence this night of debauchery, we present the world's mixed bathing champion of 1931 — the man in black — Mr. Valentine Dyall.
F.X.	VIBRANT GIANT GONG.
VAL	Allow me to correct you, little pigmy man. I am no longer the man in black; I am now the man in grey!
HARRY	What brought about this change?
VAL	A very cheap dry cleaners.
HARRY	Very well. Mr. Dyall, the floor is yours but remember, the roof, is *ours.*
VAL	Thank you, Barbara Kelly. Ladies and Gintlepong, this *is* the man in black speaking. A funny thing happened to me on my way to the theatre tonight — a steam roller ran over my head. So much for humour — and now pray allow me to tell the story of —
SPIKE	*(Scream)*
F.X.	DEEP RESONANT SPLASH.
VAL	'The Canal', ha ha ha *(goes off laughing into echo)*
ORCHESTRA	QUIET, SINISTER HORROR THEME.
SEAGOON	My name is Neddie Seagoon. I come from mixed parentage — one male, one female, and that's how it should be. My father was the famous amateur brain surgeon, Lord Valentine Seagoon.
ORD VALENTINE	Neddie was one of my adopted sons by one of my adopted wives. In 1899 I built for my family a huge mansion.
ECCLES	It was only a luxury manor — but it was home to me.
FLOWERDEW	*(nutty)* There's a cow on the roof and I am a daisy — I must be very careful of that cow . . .
ORD VALENTINE	Ha ha. My—er—children. The manor was a grim, black, foreboding place. Hanging in the eaves were myriads of red-mouthed bats that nightly danced in the dank air that arose from the oily waters of — the canal. *(Mad laughter as before)*
ECCLES	Dat's my daddie who said dat.

ORCHESTRA	CHANGE OF SCENE CHORD.
F.X.	HORSE-DRAWN HACKNEY WALKING SLOWLY. (SOUND DEADENED BY THICK FOG).
BILL	The Canal, Chapter One. Ned Seagoon returns from college.
F.X.	HORSE-DRAWN HACKNEY UP AND UNDER:—
REUBEN	Oo ooo ooo, my life, it isn't 'arf parky up on this drivin' seat — I should never have come out naked.
SEAGOON	I say, driver — have I far to go now?
REUBEN	Let's have a look — mm noo, I shouldn't think you got far to go.
F.X.	HACKNEY STOPS.
SEAGOON	Why have we stopped?
REUBEN	It's no good, mister — I can't see a thing in this fog.
SEAGOON	Never mind, I'll make it on foot — I brought one with me. Now, what's the fare?
REUBEN	See — it's Friday today, in'it?
SEAGOON	'Tis so.
REUBEN	*(to self)* See, there's the rent — school fees — instalment on the bread knife — yers, that'll be thirty-two pounds ten, mister.
SEAGOON	Villain of villains! The meter only says five shillings.
REUBEN	That meter ain't got a wife and ten kids ter keep.
SEAGOON	There, five shillings, no more. On second thoughts, here's a penny tip. The spirit of charity is not dead.
REUBEN	No, but it in't 'arf sick, mister.
SEAGOON	You jester. Farewell. Now, see — ahh yes, this is the way *(going off)* past the old blasted oak and —
F.X.	RESONANT SPLASH OF STILL DEEP WATERS.
SEAGOON	*(off)* Help!
REUBEN	Where are you, mister?
SEAGOON	*(off)* In the canal.

REUBEN	Here, catch.
F.X.	SPLASH.
REUBEN	You forgot yer bag, ha ha ha —
ORCHESTRA	MOCKING THEME. FADE INTO:—
F.X.	THREE KNOCKS ON HEAVY WOODEN DOOR.
BLOODNOCK	Coming — coming . . .
F.X.	DOOR OPENS.
BLOODNOK	Oh Neddie, it's you — in quick, before the Arabs open fire. Aeiough.
F.X.	DOOR SLAMS.
SEAGOON	Uncle Bloodnok? I thought you were in the desert.
BLOODNOK	I am.
SEAGOON	I'm sorry I'm in such a mess — I fell in the canal and I'm covered in muck, mud, grease, rubbish, tar, oil and sludge.
BLOODNOK	You know, it suits you. But how did you get past those turbanned devils of brown, the Arabs?
SEAGOON	Arabs? What are Arabs doing in Lancashire?
BLOODNOK	I can only put it down to the fog. If only Lord Kitchener would bring reinforcements. Aeiough . . .
SEAGOON	*(aside)* Mmm. Uncle Bloodnok seems to have changed.
BLOODNOK	Didn't you see them hiding behind the sand dunes?
SEAGOON	Sand dunes? Where?
BLOODNOK	Outside — I never allow them in the house. Now I must report to H.Q. Goodbye. Charge!
F.X.	HORSE GALLOPS AWAY. COCONUT SHELLS.
SEAGOON	Oh. What's happened here since I've been away at college? Anybody about? *(Calls)* Mother? Mother? Mother, I'm home.
F.X.	DOOR OPENS.
SEAGOON	Oh, mother, I'm so glad to see you. *(Big kiss)*
ELY HEADSTONE	Pardon me, sir, but I'm the butler.

SEAGOON	Oh, I'm sorry. You shouldn't wear a kilt that long, you know.
GRAVELY HEADSTONE	I have reasons for dat.
SEAGOON	I too have knobbly knees.
F.X.	DOOR OPENS. GONG.
LORD VALENTINE	Neddie!
SEAGOON	Father! You — you *are* Father, aren't you?
LORD VALENTINE	Do I have to undress?
SEAGOON	No, it's just that you've *changed* so. *(Aside)* And, dear listener, changed he had — he looked tired, weary — his eyes were sunk back in his head, they were bloodshot, watery and red-rimmed — what had caused this?
LORD VALENTINE	Neddie, we've bought a television set. But what are you doing back from school?
SEAGOON	My schooling is completed.
LORD VALENTINE	Nonsense, you've only been there forty-three years.
SEAGOON	Nevertheless, I came out top boy in the *entire* kindergarten.
LORD VALENTINE	Really? Then it's the diplomatic service for you.
FLOWERDEW	*(approach)* I'm a daisy — a beautiful daisy — please, brown cow, do not eat me — nor my friend the pansy — where are you, Ivor?
SEAGOON	Good heavens — wasn't that Uncle Rupert?
LORD VALENTINE	Yes. He's better now. Neddie, now that you're home, promise me one thing.
SEAGOON	Very well, Father, I promise!
LORD VALENTINE	Thank you. See that you keep it.
SEAGOON	Ying tong iddle I po.
LORD VALENTINE	Good. Promise me one more thing. Never — never — go near — the canal.
SEAGOON	Why not?
LORD VALENTINE	*(flaming)* Just never go near the canal, that's all. Now — you must be tired — you need rest. Eccles?
F.X.	DOOR OPENS.
ECCLES	Yer — did my daddie call me?
LORD VALENTINE	Eccles, get your things out of Neddie's room.
ECCLES	O.K.
F.X.	DOOR OPENS.
ECCLES	Come on, shoo, shoo.

F.X.	GOATS BLEATING IN A HERD — CHICKENS — COWS — DUCKS — HORSES GALLOPING OUT — CATS.
ECCLES	All out. Goodnight, Neddie — sleep well. Mind how you tread!
F.X.	DOOR SHUTS.
SEAGOON	That night I lay in bed with a clothes peg on my nose. What had happened to everybody? 'Don` go near the canal', he had said *(yawns. Goes off to sleep talking)* . . . zzzz.
F.X.	DOOR OPENS.
ORD VALENTINE	Right — he's asleep, ha ha ha. Hand me the mallet, Doctor.
EIDELBURGER	Here.
ORD VALENTINE	Right — huhhh.
F.X.	WALLOP ON BONCE.
SEAGOON	Zzzz — ooo.
BILL	*(in quick)* The Canal, Chapter Two.
ORD VALENTINE	Together — one two threeeee —
F.X.	SPLASH — BUBBLES OF BODY SINKING.
BILL	*(in quick)* The Canal, Chapter Three.
ORD VALENTINE	Hello? Lloyds? About that life insurance against drowning — yes — on my son Neddie — well — it appears to have matured — you'll bring the money round? Right. Thank you.
F.X.	RECEIVER DOWN.
ORD VALENTINE	Ha ha ha —
SPIKE	*(Off) (Long agonised scream)*
ORD VALENTINE	*(calls)* No — not tonight, dear! Forty thousand pounds, just for throwing little Neddie in the canal, ha ha —
F.X.	DOOR OPENS.
SEAGOON	*(gasping)* Father, I —
ORD VALENTINE	Neddie — you've been playing in the canal. I told you to stay away! Eccles?
ECCLES	*(off)* Yes, Daddie?
ORD VALENTINE	He's back.
ECCLES	O.K.
F.X.	DOOR OPENS.
ECCLES	All out!
F.X.	GOATS — CHICKENS — COWS — DUCKS — HORSES — CATS.

ECCLES	Here's yer clothes peg.
FLOWERDEW	I'm a daisy — father's a plum, that's why we stoned him. I hear music and there's only Max Geldray there.
MAX & ORCHESTRA	MUSIC. *(Applause)*

ORCHESTRA	SHORT DRAMATIC THEME.
BILL	The Canal, Chapter Four.
SEAGOON	These three days I've been kept locked in my room. I pass the time cutting the grass under my bed, and feeding the monkeys. At night I can hear digging in the cellar. A thought has just struck me — *(joy)* what has become of mother? Dear mother, she was like one of the family.
F.X.	DOOR OPENS.
LORD VALENTINE	In here, gentlemen.
YAKAMOTO & EIDELBURGER	Zank you. Yerserkah.
LORD VALENTINE	Neddie, I've brought two freshly-released physicians to see you, Dr. Yakamoto — and Dr. Justin Eidelburger.
SEAGOON	But there's nothing wrong with me.
EIDELBURGER	Zat's why we're here, hmm hmm hmm — za German joke. Dr. Yakamoto? Treatment!
YAKAMOTO	At once, honourable sir. Would the honourable Neddie Seagoon put both honourable feet into this delicate three-ton iron container?
LORD VALENTINE	Do as the little oriental says, Neddie.
SEAGOON	Very well, Father.
EIDELBURGER	Good. Now, we pour in ze concrete mixture, *zo!*
F.X.	CONCRETE GOING IN.
LORD VALENTINE	*(talking over it)* You see, Neddie, the doctors say — when the concrete blocks set on your feet, you won't be able to run away and play near the canal, ha ha.
ORCHESTRA	HARP ARPEGGIO (MINOR) WITH BASS CLARINET (PLAY LITTLE TUNE).
LORD VALENTINE	Hello? Lloyds? I want to add to that last policy on my son Neddie. Yes — yes, I want one that covers him in the event of his ever putting concrete blocks on his feet and throwing himself in the canal. Yes, I *know* it's not likely to happen but *just* in case.

BILL	The Canal, Chapter Five.
F.X.	SPLASH.
SEAGOON	(off) Helpppppppp. (Bubbles)
BILL	The Canal, Chapter Six. The Lock-Keeper's Lodge.
CRUN	Zzzzzoh dee de de de — mnk (mouth noises) . . . mnk — yes . . . zzzz —
SEAGOON	(off) Help!
CRUN	Mnk — yes — help, yes — mnk grmp de de de — zzzzz.
SEAGOON	(off) Help!
MINNIE	Henery? Henry, buddy? Henry, man?
CRUN	What what what what — what?
MINNIE	Henry?
CRUN	What is it, Minnie?
MINNIE	There's a gentleman in the canal, Henry.
CRUN	Oh. Thank you, Minnie. Goodnight, Min.
MINNIE	Goodnight, Hen.
	(Pause)
SEAGOON	Helppppp!
MINNIE	Henry? That gentleman is shouting, Henry.
CRUN	Oh de de — do you think he wants to pass through the lock?
MINNIE	I can't tell, Henry — but I think he must be in a submarine.
CRUN	Why?
MINNIE	He keeps going under the water.
CRUN	Really? What will they think of next, eh?
SEAGOON	Helppp!
MINNIE	He said help, Henry.
CRUN	Help? That's the distress call, isn't it?
MINNIE	Oh yes, yes — he must be drowning, Henry.

CRUN	Minnie, quick — my regulation-length lock-keeper's bathing drawers.
F.X.	DIALLING.
CRUN	Hurry, Minnie, every day is precious.
MINNIE	Hello, Ajax Laundry? Could you speed delivery of Mr. Crun's bathing drawers?
SEAGOON	Helpppp!
MINNIE	They can't deliver till next Tuesday.
CRUN	Mnn no, it's a bit risky.
F.X.	DOOR.
CRUN	*(calls)* Pardon me, sir, but can you keep afloat till next Tuesday?
SEAGOON	What's today?
CRUN	Friday.
SEAGOON	No! Helpp, I'm going down. *(Bubbles)*
CRUN	We're coming, sir — hurry, Min.
MINNIE	Coming, buddie.
CRUN	Have you turned the gas off, Min?
MINNIE	Yes, I have.
SEAGOON	Help! Helpppp!
MINNIE	I wonder who he is.
CRUN	*(calls)* What's your name, sir?
SEAGOON	*(amid bubbles)* Neddie Seagoon.
CRUN	We're pleased to meet you — my name is Crun, Henry Crun. And this is Miss Bann . . . .
SEAGOON	Helpp, bbbb, I'm going down.
CRUN	Don't do that, sir, or you'll drown. Tsu, this fog — can't see a thing.
MINNIE	Where are you, sir?
SEAGOON	In the canal.
MINNIE	He's in the canal.
CRUN	Hello, Mr. Seagoon — follow these instructions and you'll be safe. Hand me the Life-Saving Manual, Minnie — now, ready?
SEAGOON	Yes, but hurry.
CRUN	Take three dozen eggs and break into a bowl . . .
SEAGOON	Yes.
CRUN	Mix in eight ounces of castor sugar, then stir over a low gas.

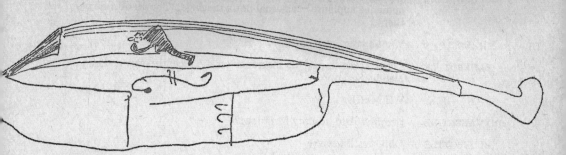

SEAGOON	I haven't got a gas stove.
MINNIE	Here, catch.
F.X.	SPLASH.
SEAGOON	Thank you.
CRUN	Right, now add four pounds of millet flour and bring the mixture to — Minnie? This isn't the Swimming Manual.
MINNIE	Oh — *(calls)* we've got the wrong book, buddy.
SEAGOON	What'll I do with all this mixture?
MINNIE	We'd better go in, Henry, it's a shame to waste all that food.
CRUN	Coming, hupppp!
F.X.	COMBINED SPLASH. SPLUTTERINGS, SHOUTS, ETC.
ORCHESTRA	SHORT LINKING CHORDS.
F.X.	KNOCK ON DOOR. DOOR OPENS.
GRAVELY HEADSTONE	Yes, sir?
BLUEBOTTLE	Oh he he, good evening to you. Is this the manor of the place where liveses the Valentine Dyall man, is dis the place, is it, man?
GRAVELY HEADSTONE	Yes.
BLUEBOTTLE	He he he. I am from the Lloyds of London, the well known insurance company — I am their junior representative. Feels in pocket, produces smart calling card.
GRAVELY HEADSTONE	Oh, come in, sir.
BLUEBOTTLE	Enter the *new* Bluebottle — the new Bluebottle wearing city gentlemen-type striped trousers and Anthony Eden homberg. (Really Dad's trilby painted black.)
GRAVELY HEADSTONE	Have you wiped your feet, sir?
BLUEBOTTLE	Yes.
GRAVELY HEADSTONE	Then where'd that mud come from?

BLUEBOTTLE	Off my shoes — ha ha he he — I made a little jokules — pauses for light audience applause — as usual not a sausinge. (Thinks of rude word for them.)
GRAVELY HEADSTONE	What's your business here?
BLUEBOTTLE	I have come to pay the insurance on the recently drowned and deaded Neddie Seagoon.
F.X.	WHOOSH.
LORD VALENTINE	(excited) Did you say insurance?
BLUEBOTTLE	Ohh, yes, I have —
LORD VALENTINE	There, just sit down and warm yourself by the candle. Here, drink this —
BLUEBOTTLE	Oh a cocktail — good health. (Gulp)
F.X.	MAMMOTH LONG RUMBLING EXPLOSION. BOOTS FALLING TO FLOOR. TEETH — ODDS AND ENDS.
BLUEBOTTLE	You rotten swine! You have nearly deaded me — look, my kneecaps have dropped four inches. Who made that cocktail?
GRAVELY HEADSTONE	Molotoff.
BLUEBOTTLE	Look what you done to my city gentleman-type suit — all the egg stains have been blowed off.
GRAVELY HEADSTONE	Is that bad?
BLUEBOTTLE	Yes, they were holding the suit together.
GRAVELY HEADSTONE	Here's the Dance of the Seven Veils.
QUARTET	MUSIC.
	(Applause)
BLUEBOTTLE	Thank you, I accept your apology. Now, Lord Valentine, the solemn business of paying out the insurance money — moves left, opens official brief case. (Not too wide, as I have my dirty laundry in one part.)
LORD VALENTINE	It's forty thousand pounds, isn't it?
BLUEBOTTLE	Yes — but it's all in pennies.
LORD VALENTINE	Forty thousand pounds in pennies? Eccles!
ECCLES	Yer, Daddie?
LORD VALENTINE	Your hat, lad.
ECCLES	O.K.
LORD VALENTINE	Just hold it there — now, Mr. Bluebottle.
BLUEBOTTLE	Right, now to . . . .
SPIKE	(Long agonised wailing heart-rending scream)
LORD VALENTINE	(answering) It's in the cabinet by the bed, dear. Carry on.

BLUEBOTTLE	He he he — what — what was that dreaded scream, sir, he heh?
LORD VALENTINE	Oh, that was my eldest thing. Ha ha — now, just count out the money.
BLUEBOTTLE	Yes — one, twopence, threepence, fourpence, fivepence —
F.X.	CLINK OF COINS BEHIND.
BILL	Chapters Seven, Eight, Nine, Ten and Eleven.
BLUEBOTTLE	*(very tired)* Four million eight hundred and thirty-two pennies ...
F.X.	CLINK.
BLUEBOTTLE	Ah he — roll on, beddy byes — four million eight hundred and thirty-three pennies — four milli —
F.X.	GREAT SACK OF PENNIES DROPPED ONTO FLOOR. THEY ROLL AND SCATTER.
ECCLES	Oh, sorry.
BLUEBOTTLE	*(cries)* Ohh! Oh! You dropped them — one penny, twopence, threepence
F.X.	DOOR OPENS.
SEAGOON	Fatherrrr.
LORD VALENTINE	*(flaming)* Neddie — you!
SEAGOON	Yes.
F.X.	DOOR OPENS.
ECCLES	Come on, all out, shoo! Shoo!
F.X.	CATTLE, ETC. (AS BEFORE).
BLUEBOTTLE	Pardon me. Did you say this was Neddie?
LORD VALENTINE	Er, yes. *(Happy)* Why, Neddie, you're safe, dear boy. Thank heaven, we thought you were drowned, didn't we, Mr. Bluebottle?
BLUEBOTTLE	He he he he, yes — well, you will not need this deaded money for him drowning. Thinks — this will save Lloyds a lot of money and who knows, a managerial job for Bluebottle. Thinks again — thanks to brains, the new wonder head-filler. Well, goodnight all. Exits left.
F.X.	WHOOSH — DOOR SHUTS.
LORD VALENTINE	Curses. Miss Throat?
THROAT	Sir?
LORD VALENTINE	That man —
THROAT	Yes?
LORD VALENTINE	Stop him.
THROAT	Right.

F.X.	WHOOSH. DOOR SLAMS.
LORD VALENTINE	*(rage)* Now, little Neddie — you've been playing in the canal again. It's got to stop.
SEAGOON.	I agree, Father.
LORD VALENTINE	Silence when you talk to me! Now, go upstairs to your room and come down *at once!* I want to talk to you.
SEAGOON	But — I can't move, these concrete blocks on my feet ...
LORD VALENTINE	We'll soon have them off. Eccles?
ECCLES	*(off)* Yup, Daddy?
LORD VALENTINE	Put these sticks of dynamite into his concrete blocks.
ECCLES	O.K., Daddie.
F.X.	FUSE STARTS TO BURN.
ECCLES	Dere! In ten seconds there'll be a dirty big —
LORD VALENTINE	Yes, yes — Neddie, wait outside in the garden will you?
SEAGOON	Yes, Father.
F.X.	DOOR OPENS AND CLOSES.
LORD VALENTINE	*(Sings)*
F.X.	DIALLING.
LORD VALENTINE	Hello, Lloyds? Yes — new life policy, please — I want to insure Neddie in the event of his ever putting concrete blocks on his feet, blowing himself up with dynamite and landing in the canal. Yes, I *know* it's not likely to happen, but *just* in case —
F.X.	EXPLOSION WHISTLE GOES UP.
BILL	Chapter Twelve.
F.X.	WHISTLE DESCENDS. SPLASH.
SEAGOON	Helppp!
BILL	The Canal, Chapter Thirteen.
F.X.	PENNIES BEING DROPPED ONTO A PILE.
BLUEBOTTLE	There, that's the lot, Lord Valentine.
LORD VALENTINE	Yes — forty thousand pounds. Poor Neddie.
BLUEBOTTLE	Yes — yes, it was funny him falling in the canal again so soon after I left — good job you ran after me, wasn't it?
LORD VALENTINE	Well, goodnight, Mr. Bluebottle — thank you for —
F.X.	DOOR OPENS. PRONOUNCED CREAK.
LORD VALENTINE	You!

F.X.	**DOOR OPENS.**
ECCLES	Shoo, git out.
F.X.	**CATTLE, ETC. (AS BEFORE).**
SEAGOON	Father!
BLUEBOTTLE	Oh, it is little Neddie — oh well, well, well. Could I have all the money back, please?
LORD VALENTINE	*No!* Hands up! All of you!
BLUEBOTTLE	Oh, he's got a gun.
LORD VALENTINE	Eccles!
ECCLES	Yes, Daddie?
LORD VALENTINE	Take these two men and chain them up in the dungeon! Ha ha ha.
ORCHESTRA	DESCENDING CHORDS.
F.X.	**HEAVY CHAINS. MANACLES.**
ECCLES	Oh di dump — dere, dere, not too tight are dey?
SEAGOON	Eccles, do you realise what Daddie's trying to do?
ECCLES	Yer, he's tryin' to keep you away from der canal because he loves you and don't want you to get drowned.
SEAGOON	No — he wants to kill us all — and that includes *you.*
ECCLES	Oooooooo.
BLUEBOTTLE	I am frighted — I don't want to be deaded yet. I haven't had my half day off this week. If you get deaded they give you the sack at Lloyds — they don't like deaded men working for dem.
SEAGOON	Shhh. Now, Eccles, undo these chains and help us capture Father before he kills us *all.*
ECCLES	O.K.
SEAGOON	Right, now this is the plan — we —
F.X.	**DUNGEON DOOR SLAMS.**
BLUEBOTTLE	Oh, look, someone has closed the dungeon door from the outside — we are trapp-ed!
LORD VALENTINE	Ha ha ha ha ha *(goes off on echo).*
SEAGOON	Curse, he's locked us in. Never mind, we'll batter the door down. Where's something with a blunt head?
ECCLES	Here y'are.
BLUEBOTTLE	Put me down, Eccles. Put me down; I shall charge the door and — and smash it down.
SEAGOON	Good man.

BLUEBOTTLE	Stand back, here I go. To matchwood I'll splinter the door — charge!
F.X.	LONG APPROACHING FOOTSTEPS (GALLOPING) GET NEARER AND FADE INTO THE DISTANCE.
BLUEBOTTLE	*(miles off)* You rotten swine — who opened the door?
ECCLES	Ha hum —
SEAGOON	Good work. Now listen, both of you — we've got to think quick.
ECCLES	Dat leaves me out!
SEAGOON	We're going to throw Father into the canal!
BILL	Chapter Fourteen.
F.X.	(OFF) SPLASH. SPLASH. SPLASH.
ECCLES	*(off)* Help!
BLUEBOTTLE	*(off)* Help!
SEAGOON	*(off)* You devil, Lord Valentine.
LORD VALENTINE	Ha ha ha ha — you didn't think you could — oooo . . .
	(Struggle)
F.X.	SPLASH.
LORD VALENTINE	Helpppp — who did that?
BILL	Last chapter.
CRUN	Hello, Lloyds — about the life insurance I took out on the four gentlemen . . .
ORCHESTRA	SIGNATURE TUNE: UP AND DOWN FOR:—
BILL	That was The Goon Show — a recorded programme featuring Peter Sellers, Harry Secombe, Spike Milligan and Valentine Dyall with the Ray Ellington Quartet and Max Geldray. The Orchestra was conducted by Wally Stott. Script by Spike Milligan. Announcer: Wallace Greenslade. The programme produced by Peter Eton.
ORCHESTRA	SIGNATURE TUNE UP TO END.
	(Applause)
MAX & ORCHESTRA	'CRAZY RHYTHM' PLAYOUT.

NAPOLEON'S PIANO

The Goon Show: No. 129 (6th Series, No. 4)
Transmission: Tuesday, 11th October 1955:
8.30—9.00 p.m. Home Service
Studio: The Camden Theatre, London

The main characters

Ned Seagoon	Harry Secombe
Grytpype-Thynne	Peter Sellers
Moriarty	Spike Milligan
Mr Henry Crun	Peter Sellers
Miss Minnie Bannister	Spike Milligan
Eccles	Spike Milligan
Major Denis Bloodnok	Peter Sellers
Justin Eidelburger	Peter Sellers
Throat	Spike Milligan
Yakamoto	Spike Milligan
Bluebottle	Peter Sellers

The Ray Ellington Quartet
Max Geldray
Orchestra Conducted by Wally Stott
Announcer: Wallace Greenslade
Script by Spike Milligan
Production by Peter Eton

Tricked into signing a contract to bring over to England the very piano that Napoleon played at Waterloo, Neddie Seagoon stows away on a boat to France. A chance meeting in the disreputable Café Tom with piano robbery specialist Justin Eidelburger seems to solve all Neddie's problems – but others, too, are after Napoleon's piano. With £10,000 at stake, the only solution is to sail the instrument back to England – a voyage fraught with peril...

BILL	This is the BBC Home Service.
GRAMS	OUTBREAK OF PEOPLE SIGHING.
BILL	Oh come, come, dear listeners — it's not that bad —
HARRY	Of course not — come, Mr. Greenslade, tell them the good news.
BILL	Ladies and gentlemen, we now have the extraordinary talking-type wireless 'Goon Show'.
GRAMS	SCREAMS OF ANGUISH. PEOPLE RUNNING AWAY.
HARRY	Mmm — is the popularity waning? Ahemm.
SPIKE	Ho ho ho, fear not, Neddie lad — we'll jolly them up with a merry laughing-type joke show. Stand prepared for the story of 'Napoleon's Piano'.
GRAMS	VERY OLD RECORD OF A PIANO SOLO (MARSEILLAISE).
SEAGOON	Napoleon's piano — the story starts in the bad old days, back in April 1955. It was early one morning. Breakfast had just been served at Beauleigh Manor — I was standing at the window, looking in. With the aid of a telescope, I was reading the paper on the breakfast table — when suddenly an advertisement caught my eye. It said —
GRYTPYPE-THYNNE	(distort) Will pay anybody five pounds to remove piano from one room to another. Apply, The Bladders, Harpyapipe, Quants.
SEAGOON	In needle nardle noo time I was at the address and with the aid of a piece of iron and a lump of wood — I made this sound.
F.X.	THREE KNOCKS WITH IRON KNOCKER ON SOLID OAK DOOR.
MORIARTY	Sapristi Knockoes — when I heard that sound I ran down the stairs and with the aid of a door knob and two hinges I made *this* sound.
F.X.	DOOR KNOB BEING HEAVILY AGITATED FOLLOWED BY FAST SQUEAKY HINGES AS DOOR OPENS.
SEAGOON	Ah, good morning.
MORIARTY	Good morning? Just a moment.
F.X.	FURIOUS DIALLING.
MORIARTY	Hello, Air Ministry Roof? Weather report. Yes? Yes, thank you.
F.X.	PHONE DOWN.
MORIARTY	You're perfectly right — it *is* a good morning.
SEAGOON	Thanks. My name is Neddie Seagoon.
MORIARTY	What a memory you have.
SEAGOON	Needle nardle noo. I've come to move the piano.
MORIARTY	(insane laugh) Come in.
SEAGOON	(insane laugh) Thanks.

MORIARTY	You must excuse the mess but we've got the Socialists in.
GRYTPYPE-THYNNE	*(approach)* Oh Moriarty, can I borrow a shoe? Mine's worn out — oh, you have company.
MORIARTY	Ahh ah — these three men are called Neddie Seagoon. He's come in answer to our ad.
GRYTPYPE-THYNNE	Ohhhh — come in — sit down. Have a gorilla.
SEAGOON	No thanks, I'm trying to give them up.
GRYTPYPE-THYNNE	Splendid. Now, Neddie, here's the money for moving the piano — there, five pounds in fivers.
SEAGOON	Five pounds for moving a piano? Ha ha — this is money for old rope.
GRYTPTPE-THYNNE	Is it? I'd have thought you'd have bought something more useful.
SEAGOON	Oh no — I have simple tastes. Now, where's this piano?
GRYTPYPE-THYNNE	Just a moment. First, would you sign this contract in which you guarantee to move the piano from one room to another for five pounds.
SEAGOON	Of course I'll sign — have you any ink?
GRYTPYPE-THYNNE	Here's a fresh bottle.
SEAGOON	*(drinks)* . . . ahhhhhhhh. Gad, I was thirsty.
MORIARTY	Sapristi Nuckoes — do you always drink ink?
SEAGOON	Only in the mating season.
MORIARTY	Shall we dance?
GRAMS	OLD 1929 SCRATCHY GUY LOMBARDO RECORD OF 'LOVER' WALTZ.
SEAGOON	You dance divinely.
GRYTPYPE-THYNNE	Next dance please! Now, Neddie, just sign the contract on the side of this horse.
SEAGOON	Certainly.
F.X.	SCRATCHING OF PEN UNDER SEAGOON AS HE SPEAKS NEXT LINE.
SEAGOON	Neddie — Seagoon — A.G.G.
MORIARTY	What's A.G.G. for?
SEAGOON	For the kiddies to ride on . . . get it? A gee-gee — ha ha ha ha — *(Agonised silence)*
GRYTPYPE-THYNNE	You're *sure* you won't have a gorilla?
SEAGOON	No thanks, I've just put one out. Now, which room is this piano in?
GRYTPYPE-THYNNE	Ahemm. It's in the Louvre.
SEAGOON	Strange place to put a piano.

GRYTPYPE-THYNNE	We refer to the Louvre Museum, Paris.
SEAGOON	What what what what what? Ahhhh, I've been tricked — ahhhh.
F.X.	**THUD OF UNCONSCIOUS BODY HITTING GROUND.**
MORIARTY	For the benefit of people without television — he's fainted.
GRYTPYPE-THYNNE	Don't waste time — just open his jacket — get the weight of his cruel wallet off his chest — mmm — found anything in his pockets?
MORIARTY	Yes — a signed photograph of Neddie Seagoon, a press cutting from the Theatre, Bolton, a gramophone record of Gigli mowing the lawn, a photo of Gigli singing, and a half share in Kim Novak.
GRYTPYPE-THYNNE	He's still out cold — see if *this* brings him round.
F.X.	**PENNY THROWN ON CONCRETE FLOOR.**

SEAGOON	Thank you, lady. *(Sings)* Comrades comrades — ever since — oh — where — where am I?
GRYTPYPE-THYNNE	England!
SEAGOON	What number?
GRYTPYPE-THYNNE	Seven A. Have a gorilla.
SEAGOON	No, they hurt my throat. Wait! *Now* I remember! You've trapped me into bringing back a piano from France for only five pounds.
GRYTPYPE-THYNNE	*You* signed the contract, Neddie — now, get that piano or we sue you for breach of contract.
SEAGOON	Ahhhhhhhh. *(Going off)*
F.X.	DOOR SLAMS.
GRYTPYPE-THYNNE	Gad, Moriarty, if he brings that piano back we'll be in the money. That piano is worth ten thousand pounds.
MORIARTY	How do you know?
GRYTPYPE-THYNNE	I've seen its bank book. Do you know, that's the very piano Napoleon played at Waterloo. With the moolah we get on that we can have a holiday. *(Sings)*
BOTH	April in Paris — we've found a Charlie.

BILL	I say — poor Neddie must have been at his wits' end! Faced with the dilemma of having to bring Napoleon's piano back from Paris, he went to the Foreign Office for advice on passports and visas.
F.X.	BITS AND PIECES DROPPING DOWN.
CRUN & MINNIE	*(Nattering away)*
CRUN	Ohh dee deee — dee, X9?
MINNIE	*(off)* X9 answering — who's that calling, buddy?
CRUN	It's me — the Foreign Secretary. Do you know where the key to the secret documents safe is?
MINNIE	Yes — it's with the charlady.
CRUN	Do you think that's wise — she has access to all the vital British secret documents.
MINNIE	She can't read them, buddy, she only speaks Russian.
CRUN	That's a bit of luck —
F.X.	KNOCKS ON DOOR.
CRUN	Ohh, that might be one of England's strolling Prime Ministers of no fixed abode.
MINNIE	Coming, Anthonyyy — coming . . .
CRUN	Tell him we're very sorry.
MINNIE	Sorry for what?
CRUN	Oh, mmm — make something up.
F.X.	DOOR OPENS.
MINNIE	Ahh, we're very sorry, Anthony, we — ohh, you're not the Prime Minister.
SEAGOON	Not yet, but it's just a matter of time. My name is Neddie Seagoon.
CRUN	Want to buy a white paper —
SEAGOON	No thanks, I'm trying to give them up.
CRUN	So are we —
SEAGOON	I want a few particulars. You see, I want to leave the country . . .
CRUN	He's going to Russia! Stop him, Min — get him!
MINNIE	Hit him, Hen . . .
GRAMS	MIX IN GREAT BATTLE. ALL STOPS SUDDENLY.
CRUN	There! Let that be a lesson to you — get out.
SEAGOON	I will, but not before I hear musical saboteur Max Geldray.
MAX & ORCHESTRA	'AIN'T MISBEHAVIN'
	(Applause)

BILL	Seagoon was confused — it seems that the cheapest method of getting to Paris was to stowaway to France on board a Channel steamer.
GRAMS	SHIP'S TELEGRAPH RINGING. SEAGULLS — WASH OF SHIP'S WAKE.
SEAGOON	Down in the dark hold I lay — alone — so I thought ...
ECCLES	(off — sings) I talk to der trees — dat's why they put me away ...
SEAGOON	The singer was a tall ragged idiot — he carried a plasticine gramophone, and wore a metal trilby.
ECCLES	Hello, shipmate. Where you goin'?
SEAGOON	Nowhere. I think it's safer to stay on the ship until we reach Calais.
ECCLES	You going to Calais?
SEAGOON	Yes.
ECCLES	What a coincidence. Dat's where the ship's going — ain't you lucky.
SEAGOON	Here — have a gorilla.
ECCLES	Oh, thanks!
GRAMS	GORILLA FIGHTING ANOTHER GORILLA (IF YOU CAN'T GET THE RIGHT SOUND TRY TWO LIONS). ALL STOPS ABRUPTLY.
ECCLES	Hey — dese gorillas are strong. Have one of my monkeys — they're milder.

"HANDSOME HARRY" (ACCORDING TO GAGS ABOUT AGE ETC.)

SEAGOON	And so for the rest of the voyage we sat quietly smoking our monkeys. At Calais I left the idiot singer. By sliding down the ship's rope in French I avoided detection. Late that night I checked into a French hotel. Next morning I sat in my room eating my breakfast when suddenly through the window a fork on the end of a long pole appeared — it tried to spear my kipper.
BLOODNOK	(off) Strained. Aeiough.
SEAGOON	Who the blazes are you, sir?

BLOODNOK	Aeioughhh — oh, oh, I'm sorry, I was fishing.
SEAGOON	Fishing? This is the thirty-fourth floor.
BLOODNOK	Oh, the river must have dropped.
SEAGOON	Who are you, sir?
BLOODNOK	I've got it on a bit of paper here — ah yes — Major Denis Bloodnok, late of the Third Disgusting Fusiliers — OBE, MT, MT, MT, MT and MT.
SEAGOON	What are all those MTs for?
BLOODNOK	I get tuppence on each of 'em — aeioughhhh.
SEAGOON	You're acting suspiciously suspicious — I've a good mind to call the manager.
BLOODNOK	Call him — I am unafraid!
SEAGOON	Mmmm — no! Why should I call him?
BLOODNOK	Then I will — manager?
F.X.	DOOR OPENS.
SPIKE	(French) Oui, monsieur?
BLOODNOK	Throw this man out.
SEAGOON	Ahhhhh. (Thrown out)
F.X.	DOOR SLAMS.
BLOODNOK	Now for breakfast — see, kippers — toast de da dee deeee. What's this coming through the window — flatten me krurker and nosh me schlappers — it's a fork, on a pole, and its trying to take the kipper off me plate — I say, who's that?
SEAGOON	I'm sorry, I was just fishing.
BLOODNOK	What, you! I've a good mind to call the manager.
SEAGOON	Go on then, call him.
BLOODNOK	No, why should I?
SEAGOON	Then I'll call him. (Watch me turn the tables, listeners.) Manager?
F.X.	DOOR OPENS.
SPIKE	Oui, Monsieur?
BLOODNOK	Throw this man out of my room.
SEAGOON	Ahhhh. (Thrown out)
F.X.	DOOR SLAMS.
SEAGOON	Alone in Paris — I went down the notorious Café Tom. Proprietor: Maurice Ponk.
GRAMS	'SOUS LES TOITS DE PARIS'.

SEAGOON	Inside, the air was filled with gorilla smoke — I was looking for a man who might specialise in piano robberies from the Louvre.
F.X.	WHOOSH.
EIDELBURGER	Gute evenung. You are looking for a man who might specialise in piano robberies from the Louvre?
SEAGOON	How do you know?
EIDELBURGER	I was listening on the radio and I heard you say it.
SEAGOON	Good — pull up a chair. Sit down.
EIDELBURGER	No thanks — I'd rather stand.
SEAGOON	Very well, stand on a chair. Garçon!
THROAT	Oui?
SEAGOON	Two glasses of English port-type cooking sherry, and vite.
THROAT	Two glasses of sherry and vite coming up.
SEAGOON	Now — name?
EIDELBURGER	I am Justin Eidelburger.
SEAGOON	Oh. Have a gorilla.
EIDELBURGER	No zanks — I only smoke baboons.
SEAGOON	This piano we must steal, it's the one Napoleon played at Waterloo.
EIDELBURGER	That will be a very sticky job.
SEAGOON	Why?
EIDELBURGER	It's just been varnished — he ha, zer German joke.
SEAGOON	Zer English silence.
EIDELBURGER	Now, Mr. Snzeegroon — meet me outside the Louvre at midnight on the stroke of two.
SEAGOON	Right.
SEAGOON	True to my word, I was there dead on three.
EIDELBURGER	You're late.
SEAGOON	I'm sorry — my legs were slow.
EIDELBURGER	You must buy another pair. Zis here is my oriental assistant, Yakamoto.
YAKAMOTO	I am very honoured to meet you. Oh boy.
SEAGOON	What does this oriental creep know about piano thieving?
EIDELBURGER	Nothing — he's just here to lend colour to the scene. Now, Neddie, this is a map-plan of the Louvre and the surrounding streets.
F.X.	LONG UNFOLDING.

SEAGOON	You take one end.
F.X.	UNFOLDING. THE MAP BEING UNFOLDED CONTINUES FOR A WHOLE MINUTE.
SEAGOON	It's big, isn't it?
EIDELBURGER	*(in the distance)* Yes, it is! This bit here shows the Rue de la Paix.
SEAGOON	Good heavens, you're miles away — walk straight up that street — take the second on the left — I'll be waiting for you.
F.X.	TAXI PULLS UP.
EIDELBURGER	I took a taxi — it was too far. Now — we disperse and meet again in the Hall of Mirrors, when the clock strikes twinge. At midnight we strike.

F.X.	BIG BEN STRIKES TWELVE — AT VARYING SPEEDS.
SEAGOON	Shhhhhh.
EIDELBURGER	Is that you, Seagoon?
SEAGOON	Yes.
EIDELBURGER	Good.
F.X.	HAND BELL.
BILL	*(French)* Every bodee out, closing time — everyone back to zere own bed.
SEAGOON	Quick, hide behind this pane of glass.
EIDELBURGER	But you can see through it.
SEAGOON	Not if you close your eyes.
EIDELBURGER	Gerblunden, you're right — are all your family clever?
SEAGOON	Only the Crustaceans.

BILL	Everybody out — and that goes for you idiots with your eyes shut behind that sheet of glass.
SEAGOON	You fool, you can't see us.
BILL	Yes, I can — get out or I'll call the police.
EIDELBURGER	Why, you anti-Bismark swine, I shoot you.
SEAGOON	No, not through the glass — you'll break it. First I'll make a hole in it.
F.X.	PANE OF GLASS SHATTERING TO PIECES.
SEAGOON	*Now* shoot through that.
F.X.	PISTOL SHOT.
BILL	You've killed me — now I'll get the sack. Ooooooo — ohhhh — ohhhhh — I die — I fall to the ground — ahhh meee — ahh my — ohhh ohhh I die, killed by death!
SEAGOON	Never mind — swallow this tin of Lifo guaranteed to return you to life — recommended by all corpses and Wilfred Pickles. Forward, Ray Ellington and his music!
QUARTET	'BLOODSHOT EYES'
	(Applause)

ELLINGTON
(DOWN THE
SOCK MINE)

BILL	Part Two — in which our heroes are discovered creeping up to the piano.
EIDELBURGER	Shhh, Neddie — there's someone under Napoleon's piano, trying to lift it by himself.
SEAGOON	He must be mad.
ECCLES	*(sings)* I talk to der trees . . .
SEAGOON	I was right. Eccles, what are you doing out after feeding time?
ECCLES	I signed a contract that fooled me into taking dis piano back to England.
SEAGOON	What? You must be an idiot to sign a contract like that — now, help me get this piano back to England. Together, lift!
OMNES	*(Grunts, groans)*
SEAGOON	No, no, it's too heavy — put it down.

ECCLES	Here, it's lighter when you let go.
SEAGOON	I have an idea — we'll saw the legs off. Eccles, give me that special piano leg saw that you just happen to be carrying. Now . . .
F.X.	SAWING.
ECCLES	*(sings over sawing)* I talk to der trees — dat's why dey put me away —
SEAGOON	There! I've sawn all four legs off.
EIDELBURGER	Strange — first time I've known of a piano with four legs.
ECCLES	Hey — I keep falling down — ohhhhhhh.
SEAGOON	Sorry, Eccles — here, swallow this tin of Leggo, the wonder leg-grower recommended by all good centipedes.
BILL	Sweating and struggling, they managed to get Napoleon's piano into the cobbled court.
SEAGOON	*(dry)* Which was more than Napoleon ever did.
BLOODNOK	Halt — hand over le piano in the name of France!
SEAGOON	Bloodnok, take off that kilt, we know you're not French.
BLOODNOK	One step nearer and I'll strike with this fork on the end of a pole.
SEAGOON	You do, and I'll attack with this kipper.
BLOODNOK	I've a good mind to call the manager.
SEAGOON	Call the manager.
BLOODNOK	No, why should I —
SEAGOON	Very well, I'll call him (I'll get him this time). Manager?
F.X.	DOOR OPENS.
SPIKE	Oui, Monsieur?
SEAGOON	Throw this man out.
SPIKE	*(Raspberry)*
F.X.	DOOR SHUTS.
SEAGOON	Nurse? Put the screens around that bed.
BLOODNOK	Seagoon, you must let me have that piano — you see, I foolishly signed a contract that forces me to —
SEAGOON	Yes, yes, we know — we're all in the same boat. We have no money, so the only way to get the piano back to England is to float it back. All together into the English Channel — hurl.
F.X.	PAUSE — SPLASH.
SEAGOON	All aboard — cast off.
ORCHESTRA	SEASCAPE MUSIC.

GRAMS   HEAVY SEAS. GULLS.

SEAGOON   The log of Napoleon's Piano. December the third — Second week in English Channel. Very seasick — no food — no water. Bloodnok down with the lurgi. Eccles up with the lark.

BLOODNOK   Ohhh — Seagoon — take over the keyboard, I can't steer any more.

SEAGOON   Eccles? Take over the keyboard.

ECCLES   I can't. I haven't brought my music.

SEAGOON   You'll have to busk for the next three miles.

BLOODNOK   Wait! Great galloping crabs, look in the sky.

GRAMS   HELICOPTER.

BLOODNOK   It's a recording of a helicopter — saved!

SEAGOON   By St. George — saved — yes. For those of you who haven't got television, they're lowering a man on a rope.

BLUEBOTTLE   Yes, it is I, Sea Ranger Blunebontle. Signals applause.

GRAMS   APPLAUSE.

BLUEBOTTLE   Cease — I have drunk my fill of the clapping.

SEAGOON   Little stinking Admiral, you have arrived in the nick of time.

BLUEBOTTLE	Silence — I must do my duty — hurriedly runs up cardboard Union Jack. I now claim this island for the British Empire and Lord Beaverbrook, the British patriot — thinks, I wonder why he lives in France. Three cheers for the Empire — hip hip hooray — hip hip . . .
SEAGOON	Have you come to save us?
BLUEBOTTLE	Hooray! Rockall is now British — cements in brass plate — steps back to salute.
GRAMS	SPLASH.
BLUEBOTTLE	Help! I'm in the dreaded drowning-type water.
SEAGOON	Here, grab this fork on the end of a pole.
BLUEBOTTLE	It's got a kipper on it.
SEAGOON	Yes, you *must* keep your strength up.
BLUEBOTTLE	But I'm drowning.
SEAGOON	There's no need to go hungry as well. Take my hand.
BLUEBOTTLE	Why? Are you a stranger in paradise?
SEAGOON	Heave . . . for those without television, I've pulled him back on the piano.
BLUEBOTTLE	Piano? This is not a piano — this is Rockall.

SEAGOON	This is Napoleon's piano.
BLUEBOTTLE	No, no — this is Rockall — we have tooked it because it is in the area of the rocket testing range.
SEAGOON	I've never heard . . .
F.X.	ROCKET WHOOSH. EXPLOSION.
BILL	What do you think, dear listeners — were they standing on Rockall or was it Napoleon's piano? Send your suggestions to anybody but us. For those who would have preferred a happy ending, here it is.
F.X.	DOOR OPENS.
HARRY	Gwendeloine?? Gwendoline.
PETER	John, John darling —
HARRY	I've found work, darling. I've got a job.
PETER	Oh John, I'm so glad for you — what is it?
HARRY	All I've got to do is to move a piano from one room to another.
MORIARTY	*(Mad laugh)*
ORCHESTRA	SIGNATURE TUNE: UP AND DOWN FOR:
BILL	That was The Goon Show — a BBC recorded programme featuring Peter Sellers, Harry Secombe and Spike Milligan with the Ray Ellington Quartet and Max Geldray. The Orchestra was conducted by Wally Stott. Script by Spike Milligan. Announcer: Wallace Greenslade. The programme produced by Peter Eton.
ORCHESTRA	SIGNATURE TUNE UP TO END.
	(Applause)
MAX & ORCHESTRA	'CRAZY RHYTHM' PLAYOUT.

FOILED BY PRESIDENT FRED

The Goon Show: No. 132 (6th Series, No. 7)
Transmission: Tuesday, 1st November 1955:
8.30—9.00 p.m. Home Service
Studio: The Garrick Theatre, London

The main characters

Gas Meter Inspector Ned Seagoon	Harry Secombe
Mr Henry Crun	Peter Sellers
Miss Minnie Bannister	Spike Milligan
Major Denis Bloodnok	Peter Sellers
Moriarty	Spike Milligan
Eccles	Spike Milligan
Bluebottle	Peter Sellers
Grytpype-Thynne	Peter Sellers
General Aston Villa	Peter Sellers
Manager	Spike Milligan

The Ray Ellington Quartet
Max Geldray
Orchestra Conducted by Wally Stott
Announcer: Wallace Greenslade
Script by Spike Milligan
Production by Peter Eton

Two poverty-stricken foreign devils, Señor Grytpype-Thynne and Count Moriaty, skint to the wide, are one day watching TV in their chicken-run in King's Cross back alley when Neddie Seagoon arrives to empty the gas meter. Staggering under the weight of a sack bursting with coppers, he foolishly accepts an offer to join them in a quarter bottle of Maurice Ponk's doped apple-jack. While still reeling from the effects of this vicious carousal he is introduced to Gladys Knees, a diaphanous spy and part-time dustwoman, who induces him to sink further into the abyss of vice by partaking of a portion of heavily loaded smoked haddock. Before he lapses into unconsciousness Ned overhears the mysterious Count Jim booking reservations for South America, and he realises that once more he has become enmeshed in the plot to kidnap President Fred and relieve him of his historic portion of the International Christmas Pudding...

Peter's picture D
Blodwen as Villa.
Harry as Gasman.

BILL	This is the BBC Home Service. And candidly, I'm fed up with it.
HARRY	Have a care there, Wallace, otherwise I'll be forced to speak to John Snagge.
BILL	My dear fellow, everybody has to be forced to speak to John Snagge.
HARRY	Come, curb those biting cynicisms and permit me to present the highly esteemed Goon Show.
GRAMS	AEOLIAN CLARINET (OR OLD DANCE MUSIC RECORD)
SPIKE	Stop that sinful music! Secombe? Take off those carbon-paper plus fours and listen to the story entitled — 'In Honour Bound'.
ORCHESTRA	TRADITIONAL ENGLISH HERO THEME.
SEAGOON	My name is Neddie Seagoon. I was a gas meter inspector. It all began the day of the annual general board meeting of the South Balham Gas Board.
F.X.	MURMURS — GAVEL.
CRUN	Gentlemen — I have here the books for the — mnk — financial year — mnk — just ended — mnk — mnk — and by the look of them gas is here to stay. I am glad to say that the South Balham Gas Colossus has made a gross profit of no less than three pounds twelve shillings and nine.
GRAMS	CLAPPING.
CRUN	It proves that hard work pays. Now, I'll read the vital balance sheet. Credits — sales of gas, eighteen pounds. Expenses — one bag of coke, eight and sixpence; electric fire for office heating, two pounds, eleven and fourpence; replacing light bulbs in Gas Board's premises, thirteen shillings and tenpence; saxophone lessons for Chairman's wife, three pounds, eight shillings and ninepence . . .
MINNIE	*(off)* Do we have to pay for saxophone lessons, buddy?
CRUN	Ah — yes — you never know when it comes in useful — mnk — mnk — next we have the — oh! — ah! — oh! I overlooked an entry here — an outstanding debt of four pounds, nineteen shillings and sixpence!
GRAMS	SENSATION.
CRUN	Don't worry! I shall set this right at once. *(Calls)* Ned Seagoon?
F.X.	DOOR OPENS.
SEAGOON	Gas meter inspector Seagoon reporting for duty, sir.
CRUN	Seagoon, go to this address and — mnk — serve them a seven-day final notice.
SEAGOON	Yes sir. What's this? President Fred, Casa Rosa, Avenida Varest, Buenos Aires, Argentina? Argentina? That's South America.
CRUN	Ohhoho — is it? Then you'd better borrow the Gas Board's bicycle.
SEAGOON	But sir, it's overseas.
CRUN	*(angry)* What's our bicycle doing overseas?

SEAGOON	No, no. I mean *Argentina* is overseas. How can I get there on a bicycle?
CRUN	Well, you must have it waterproofed.
SEAGOON	Oh, thank you, sir. I hadn't thought of that. Goodbye, sir.
OMNES	Goodbye — Ta ta.
BILL	Dear listeners, you doubtless are wondering how it is that the South Balham Gas Board supplies gas to Argentina. It was thanks to the enterprise of a British Major who, in 1939, shipped a cylinder of gas there.
SEAGOON	Yes, on arrival in Argentina it was this man I contacted.
ORCHESTRA	BLOODNOK THEME.
GRAMS	RECORD OF FLAMENCO GUITAR.
BLOODNOK	Ah! Oh! The heat! Gladys?
RAY	Si, señor?
BLOODNOK	Turn off one of those women and put some more ice on the fire — ah!
F.X.	KNOCK ON DOOR.
BLOODNOK	*(suspicious)* Who's there?
SEAGOON	*(off)* Ned Seagoon, South Balham Gas Board.
BLOODNOK	Quick! Burn the books. Tear up those revolting postcards. Chase those women out of my room. Take all those 'For Sale' signs off the furniture and help me get the floor back under this carpet. *(Makes huge effort)* Come in!
F.X.	DOOR OPENS.
SEAGOON	Good morning.
BLOODNOK	I'm sorry your journey's all been wasted. I posted the account books back to Balham this morning. Goodbye.
F.X.	DOOR SLAMS. LOUD KNOCKING.
BLOODNOK	You can't come in. I'm in the bath.
SEAGOON	*(off)* What are you doing in the bath?
BLOODNOK	I'm — I'm watching television.
SEAGOON	*(off)* What's showing?
BLOODNOK	My dear fellow — nothing. I've got a towel round me.
F.X.	DOOR OPENS.
SEAGOON	Look here, Major, enough of this tomfoolery.
BLOODNOK	Do you play the saxophone?
SEAGOON	No. I'm here to deliver a final demand notice to a President Fred — how do I contact him?

BLOODNOK	Come to the window, lad . . .
F.X.	**WINDOW RAISED. DISTANT SHOTS AND SOUNDS OF WARFARE.**
BLOODNOK	That white house in the square is President Fred's headquarters.
SEAGOON	But how can I get through that hail of bullets?
BLOODNOK	Be outside the back door at midnight. I shall send a man to guide you.
SEAGOON	Very well. But remember — if I'm not back within seven days, don't hesitate to cut off their gas supply. Farewell!
F.X.	**DOOR SLAMS. PHONE UP.**
BLOODNOK	Hello, Moriarty?
MORIARTY	Yes.
BLOODNOK	Listen, there's a Charlie from Balham coming over to collect a gas bill from President Fred. It's only three pounds, twelve shillings and ninepence.

MORIARTY	Bloodnok, that money was paid to *you* last month.
BLOODNOK	I know, but I don't want any trouble with the South Balham Gas fellows. Be a good feller and settle it up.
MORIARTY	Sapristi galamnackos! How *can* we pay him? President Fred has vanished with all the money. I think you'd better come over here at once.
BLOODNOK	Very well. I'll pause only for Max Geldray.
MAX & ORCHESTRA	'HAVE YOU EVER BEEN LONELY'.

(Applause)

SEAGOON	That night at midnight I waited in a specially darkened doorway for the coming of the stranger who was to guide me on my perilous mission. I was so heavily disguised that not even my own mother would have recognised me.
MOTHER	Good evening, Neddie.
SEAGOON	Good evening, mum. *(Embarrassed cough)* But wait! Who is this approaching, wearing an anthracite tie, lead waistcoat, with an electric guitar plugged into the tram lines?
ECCLES	Ahem — psst!
SEAGOON	Are you pssting at me?
ECCLES	Yeah. You Neddie Seagoon?
SEAGOON	I am.
ECCLES	Been waiting long?
SEAGOON	Yes.
ECCLES	Who for?
SEAGOON	You, you idiot. Now, how do I get through the firing line to President Fred's headquarters?
ECCLES	Go straight up that road there.
SEAGOON	But they're shooting down it.
ECCLES	Oh. Don't go that way. Take this road here. They're not shooting down that.
SEAGOON	That road doesn't lead to it.
ECCLES	No, don't take that one.
	(Pause)
SEAGOON	Any other ideas?
ECCLES	Do you play the saxophone?

SEAGOON	No.
ECCLES	Well — I'd better be getting along now.
SEAGOON	Don't go. The sewers! That's how we'll get there. Quick. Down this manhole.
F.X.	MANHOLE COVER. TWO SPLASHES. WADING (CONTINUES:—)
SEAGOON	*(proud)* Now — I'm going to roll up my trousers.
ECCLES	Why?
SEAGOON	I've got nice legs. Wait! What's that ahead?
ECCLES	It's a head.
SEAGOON	Yes, but whose it is?
BLUEBOTTLE	It is mine, my capting.
SEAGOON	Who are you, little cardboard-clad frogman?
BLUEBOTTLE	I will give you a musical clue. Close your eyes. Moves right, picks up flannel zither. *(Sings)* Plunka-plunka-plunka-plunk . . . etc. *('Harry Lime')*
ECCLES	I know. The Man from Laramie.
BLUEBOTTLE	*(heartbroken)* You rotten swine, you. I'm not the Laramie man. I'm the Harry Lime-type man. Goes into second chorus. *(Sing as before)*
SEAGOON	Save that lovely voice, little widget. Tonight is not the Harry Lime game. Tonight is the South American President Fred game.
BLUEBOTTLE	Oh! Do not go. Wait for me. Quickly throws away silly zither, makes brown paper lariat, reverses Mum's old bloomers to make cowboy trousers and picks up hair and fibre banjo. Olé! Am ready for new game. Ride, vaquero, ride!
SEAGOON	Well done, little thrice-adolescent hybrid. Lead me to President Fred's headquarters and this quarter of liquorice all-sorts is yours.
BLUEBOTTLE	Oooh! Licorish! Thinks. I must be careful how many of these I eat. Right, Captain, quick — jump into this cardboard bootbox. Hurriedly wraps up captain in brown paper parcel labelled "Explosives" and stuffs him through headquarters letter box. Jumps on to passing dustcart and exits left to buy bowler before price goes up. Thinks — that wasn't a very big part for Bluebottle.
BILL	By the magic of inconsequence the scene now changes to the Suspicious Parcels Testing Chamber in President Fred's headquarters.
MORIARTY	Grytpype, this mysterious parcel has just arrived by mysterious parcel post — mysteriously.
GRYTPYPE-THYNNE	Right, Moriarty. Steam the stamp off and cash it.
MORIARTY	Sapristi Muchos! I don't like the expression on this parcel's label. I wonder what's in it.
F.X.	PHONE RINGS. RECEIVER UP.

GRYTPYPE-THYNNE	Hello?
SEAGOON	*(distort)* I'll tell you what's in the parcel. It's me, gas meter Inspector Neddie Seagoon, South Balham Gas Board. You have seven days to pay a gas bill of three pounds, twelve and nine.
GRYTPYPE-THYNNE	Um! Do you play the saxophone?
SEAGOON	*(distort)* No. Now listen, you have seven days to pay. You can post your cheque to me care of this parcel.
F.X.	PHONE DOWN.
GRYTPYPE-THYNNE	Mmm! Moriarty, hand me that forty-ton steam hammer.
F.X.	PSST! THUD! PHONE RINGS AND RECEIVER UP.
SEAGOON	*(distort)* Ow!
F.X.	RECEIVER DOWN.
GRYTPYPE-THYNNE	Yes — Moriarty, make a hole in the parcel, insert the nozzle of this hose and turn it on — so!
F.X.	RUNNING WATER. PHONE RINGS AND RECEIVER UP.
GRYTPYPE-THYNNE	Hello?
SEAGOON	*(through water)* Bobbleobbleobbleobble — plumber!
F.X.	PHONE DOWN.
GRYTPYPE-THYNNE	That'll do, Moriarty. I think he's had enough. Open it.
F.X.	PAPER TORN.
SEAGOON	Thank heaven you've arrived. The roof was leaking. Now then — what about this gas bill? President Fred owes the South Balham Gas Board three pounds, twelve shillings and ninepence.
GRYTPYPE-THYNNE	Oh — I tell you what. Go down to the basement and read the meter and make sure.
SEAGOON	Right. Come, Eccles —
F.X.	DOOR SHUTS.
GRYTPYPE-THYNNE	Good. That gives us a breathing space. I say, how empty the room is without him.
F.X.	BACKGROUND SHOOTING.
MORIARTY	Sapristi — the counter-revolutionaries with tanks are attacking.
GRYTPYPE-THYNNE	We've got to evacuate.
MORIARTY	Why?
GRYTPYTE-THYNNE	The rent's too high here. Pack the floor. We're leaving.
F.X.	DOOR SHUTS. DOOR BROKEN DOWN. SHOTS.

"OMNES: MURMUR"

OMNES	*(Shouts)*
GENERAL ASTON VILLA	Well, the cowardly swines have run away. They are frightened of Il Heneral Aston Villa. Run up my personal flag. Ssh! Someone's coming upstairs.
F.X.	**DOOR OPENS.**
SEAGOON	Right, gentlemen, I've checked the meter, and the bill is exactly four pounds.
GENERAL ASTON VILLA	What are you talking about, you miserable English creep?
SEAGOON	Come, come, Mr. Grytpype, you can't fool the South Balham Gas Board with those childish disguises and silly changes of voice. Four pounds, please.
GENERAL ASTON VILLA	There is some mistake, señor. We have just taken possession here this very minute. We only just lit the gas.
SEAGOON	Good heavens, I'm dreadfully sorry. In that case you couldn't have used more than a therm or two. I'll go down and read the meter again. Excuse me . . .
F.X.	**DOOR CLOSES.**
GENERAL ASTON VILLA	Now — when he comes up — pay the bill — then keel heem.

F.X.	**BURST OF FIRING.**
OBREGON	Queeck! The President Fredists are attacking.
GENERAL ASTON VILLA	Everybody retreat.
F.X.	**GENERAL STAMPEDE OUT AND DOOR CLOSES.**
	(Pause)
F.X.	**DOOR OPENS.**
GRYTPYPE-THYNNE	Well done, Moriarty. What a beautiful counter-attack. We couldn't have continued to hold *their* headquarters anyway. Three pounds, ten shillings a week? Impossible!
F.X.	**DOOR OPENS.**
SEAGOON	Well, gentlemen, I've read the meter. And you were quite right. You'd only put on one more therm — one and six please.
GRYTPYPE-THYNNE	Right. Here's a photograph of two shillings.
SEAGOON	Thank you. And here's a photograph of sixpence — change.
GRYTPYPE-THYNNE	Can't you do it in coppers?
SEAGOON	By all means — here's a photograph of sixpence in coppers.
GRYTPYPE-THYNNE	Thank you.
SEAGOON	No — wait! It's you back again! You've cheated me. You're the people who owe the three pounds, twelve shillings and ninepence.
GRYTPYPE-THYNNE	That's President Fred's responsibility. Go and see him. Room 509.
SEAGOON	I will. But wait! Who is this approaching, riding a kilted monkey and carrying a mackintosh sackbut? It's Ray Ellington!
QUARTET	**'BIRTH OF THE BLUES'.**
	(Applause)

BILL	Here for idiots is a résumé. The revolution so far.
F.X.	SHOOTING.
BILL	Thank you. Chapter Two.

F.X.	KNOCKING ON THE DOOR.
BLOODNOK	Heavens-o! El knocko on the door-o. Come in-o.
F.X.	DOOR OPENS.
SEAGOON	Good morning, President Fred Peron. I've come to collect — wait a minute. You don't look like President Fred Peron.
BLOODNOK	What a coincidence! Neither do you!
SEAGOON	But I'm not supposed to be him.
BLOODNOK	Oh! So that's your excuse, is it? By the way, do you play the saxophone?
SEAGOON	No.
BLOODNOK	I'll give you a lesson.
SAXOPHONE	SOLO — 'VALSE VANITE'.
SEAGOON	Stop that! I'm convinced you're not President Fred. You're Major Bloodnok.
BLOODNOK	Nonsense. And you can soon find out. 'Phone him on the telefonico at this number-o: three-o nine-o.
SEAGOON	By gad, I will . . .
F.X.	RECEIVER UP. DIALLING.
SEAGOON	(over) I'll soon call this cunning bluff.
F.X.	PHONE RINGS.
BLOODNOK	Excuse me a moment.
F.X.	PHONE UP.

BLOODNOK	Hello. Three-o nine-o here.
SEAGOON	Who's that speaking?
BLOODNOK	Major Denis Bloodnok.
SEAGOON	Oh! I'm sorry. There's a man here whom I've accused of being you.
BLOODNOK	Why?
SEAGOON	He's your living image. He even sounds like you.
BLOODNOK	Nonsense — goodbye —
F.X.	PHONE DOWN.
BLOODNOK	*(to Seagoon)* Well, you doubter? You see?
SEAGOON	I'm sorry. But if *you're* President Fred, there's a gas bill here which now stands at four pounds.
BLOODNOK	Oh! Right, I'll pay you. Here's a photograph of a four pound note.
SEAGOON	Thank you. Now I can report back to Major Bloodnok, 'Mission completed. Gas bill paid in full'.
F.X.	DOOR SLAMS.
BLOODNOK	Good, he's gone.
	(Pause)
F.X.	DOOR OPENS.
MORIARTY	Ah! Bloodnok! You got rid of him, then. Splendid. And we for our part — we've got rid of President Fred Peron.
BLOODNOK	You mean . . . ?
MORIARTY	Yes. He gave us all his money to smuggle him out of the country.

BLOODNOK	Well done. Now to divide his fifty million.
MORIARTY	Yes. I have it here in this red sack.
BLOODNOK	Good. We'll split evenly. I'll take the money and you take the sack.
MORIARTY	No. Why should I get the lion's share? You have the sack and I'll take the money.
BLOODNOK	Listen, Moriarty. Let us settle this thing amicably.
F.X.	SHOT.
MORIARTY	Oh, Sapristi Nuckos! Dead!
F.X.	THUD.
BLOODNOK	Good heavens! That pistol was loaded. Poor Moriarty. I wonder if he played the saxophone. Taxi!
F.X.	TAXI DRIVES OFF.
	(Pause)
F.X.	DOOR OPENS.
TPYPE-THYNNE	Has he gone?
MORIARTY	Yes. He swallowed the bait, hook, line and sinker. I gave him a pistol with a blank cartridge and he took the red sack full of the forged banknotes.
TPYPE-THYNNE	Splendid. I've got the genuine money here in this *blue* sack. Now, you go to the airport, Moriarty, and buy two air tickets.
MORIARTY	Right.
F.X.	WHOOSH. DOOR SHUTS.
TPYPE-THYNNE	Fifty million, eh? *(Sings softly)* Christmas in Capri, millions of moulah ...

2

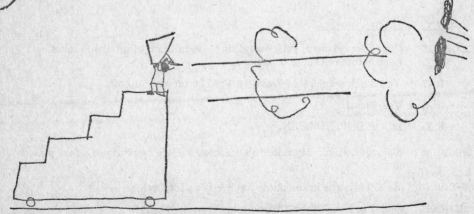

F.X.	DOOR OPENS.
ECCLES	Hello, Mr. Grytpype. I see you got that old red sack full of those forged notes ready to fool old Bloodnok, then. That was a good idea of yours having me pack those two sacks. Where's the *blue* sack with the *real* stuff?
GRYTPYPE-THYNNE	This *is* the blue one.
ECCLES	Oh! That man was right then.
GRYTPYPE-THYNNE	What man?
ECCLES	That oculist fellow who said I was colour-blind.
GRYTPYPE-THYNNE	You mean Bloodnok has the *real* money?
ECCLES	Yeah.
GRYTPYPE-THYNNE	Moriarty! Quick!
F.X.	WHOOSH! WHOOSH!
ECCLES	*(sings)* I talk to der trees — dat's why . . . *(etc.)*
F.X.	DOOR OPENS.
BLUEBOTTLE	Has Mr. Grytpype gone, Eccles?
ECCLES	Yup. Yup. *(Sings)*
BLUEBOTTLE	And left us the blue sack with all the real money?
ECCLES	Yup. *(Sings)*
ECCLES & BLUEBOTTLE	Ha. Ha. Ha.
BLUEBOTTLE	Oh, I like this game, don't you, Eccles?
ECCLES	Yup, it's fine — fine.
BOTH	*(sings)* Christmas in Capri, plenty of money . . .
	(Fade)
F.X.	DOOR OPENS.
BLOODNOK	*(breathlessly)* Juan! Pack everything. I've millions of moulah. I must leave before Neddie gets back . . .
RAY	You'd better take that President Fred Peron make up off.
BLOODNOK	Yes, there!
F.X.	DOOR BURSTS OPEN.
SEAGOON	Major Bloodnok My mission's completed. Here's a photo of a four pound note.
BLOODNOK	Wait! This note in the photograph — it's a forgery!
SEAGOON	Gad, I've been tricked! Bloodnok, I'll go right back!

F.X.	DOOR SLAMS.
BLOODNOK	(hums) Christmas in Capri — let's count the moolah.
F.X.	DOOR OPENS.
MORIARTY	Hands up!
BLOODNOK	Ah! Great thundering widgets of Kludge! Put down that double-action hydraulic-recoil eighteen-inch Howitzer.
MORIARTY	No. It belonged to my mother.
BLOODNOK	What do you want?
MORIARTY	Give me that sack of money.
BLOODNOK	Come, come, Moriarty. Old friends mustn't fall out.
MORIARTY	Very well, we'll settle this amicably.
BLOODNOK	How?
MORIARTY	Like this.
F.X.	SHOT.
BLOODNOK	Ah! Shot through me gaiters!
MORIARTY	Got him.
F.X.	DOOR OPENS.
GRYTPYPE-THYNNE	Is he dead?
MORIARTY	Yes.
F.X.	SHOT.
MORIARTY	Ooooh! Shot in the kringe!
F.X.	THUD.
GRYTPYPE-THYNNE	Got him!
F.X.	DOOR OPENS.
SEAGOON	Grytpype!
GRYTPYPE-THYNNE	Hello, Neddie.
SEAGOON	What are these men lying on the floor for?
GRYTPYPE-THYNNE	We haven't got any carpets.
SEAGOON	Eccles told me that Bloodnok ran off with a red sack full of banknotes, believing them to be real.
GRYTPYPE-THYNNE	And — weren't they?
SEAGOON	No. The real ones are with Eccles.
F.X.	WHOOSH. DOOR SHUTS. (PAUSE.) DOOR OPENS.

ECCLES	Hullo. Has he gone?
SEAGOON	Yes.
ECCLES	Fine, fine, fine. You know, I'm not really colour-blind at all. I only said that to fool Bluebottle. That *blue* sack you're holding is full of the *real* stuff.
SEAGOON	Blue? This is a *red* sack.
ECCLES	Ooooh! Then you got the wrong stuff. Bluebottle's got the real stuff.
SEAGOON	Then I must find him and collect the Gas Board's four pounds from President Fred's treasure. Farewell.
F.X.	DOOR SHUTS.
	(Pause)
F.X.	DOOR OPENS.
BLUEBOTTLE	Has he gone, Eccles?
ECCLES	Yup, yup.
BLUEBOTTLE	And now we have both sacks — the red one and the blue one. Heehee! This is a good game. Eccles, which sack has the *real* money?
ECCLES	The blue one.
BLUEBOTTLE	Then we will split it fifty-fifty. You take the red one and I'll take the blue one.
ECCLES	Fine, fine.
BLUEBOTTLE	And you're sure you're not colour-blind?
ECCLES	No, no.

BLUEBOTTLE	Well, goodbye Eccles..
F.X.	DOOR SHUTS.
ECCLES	Goodbye, Redbottle.
BILL	Three weeks later, at the head office of the South Balham Gas Board.
F.X.	KNOCK ON DOOR.
MANAGER	Come in.
F.X.	DOOR OPENS.
VIOLIN	'HEARTS AND FLOWERS'.
MANAGER	Seagoon, put that blasted violin down and get up off your knees. Here — I'll hold that celluloid baby.
	MUSIC OUT.
SEAGOON	Please sir, I know I failed to collect that bill, but — couldn't I have my old job back?
MANAGER	I'm sorry, it's gone. Allow me to introduce our new gas meter inspector, Balham area — President Fred.
BLOODNOK	Ah! Pleased to meet you.
SEAGOON	Oh no!
ORCHESTRA	LINK.
BILL	Meantime, on the Isle of Capri . . .
GUITAR	MUSIC ACCOMPANIMENT.
ECCLES	(hums) "O Sole Mio" etc . . . (Calls) Hey, Manager! My bill!

GRYTPYPE-THYNNE	Yes, sir. Let me see now, sir. Egg on toast and small pot of tea — that makes just fifty million pesos.
ECCLES	Oh, that's okay. I've got it all here in this blue sack.
GRYTPYPE-THYNNE	But that's a red sack.
ECCLES	Oooh!
ORCHESTRA	SIGNATURE TUNE: UP AND DOWN FOR:—
BILL	Stop! Stop, please!
	MUSIC OUT.
BILL	If the cast will just gather round, the BBC cashier will pay them for the last overseas repeat in pesos from this blue sack.
HARRY	But that's a red sack.
PETER	Blue.
SPIKE	It's green.
ORCHESTRA	SIGNATURE TUNE: UP AND DOWN FOR:—
BILL	That was The Goon Show — a BBC recorded programme featuring Peter Sellers, Harry Secombe and Spike Milligan with the Ray Ellington Quartet and Max Geldray. The orchestra was conducted by Wally Stott. Script by Spike Milligan. Announcer Wallace Greenslade. The programme was produced by Peter Eton.
ORCHESTRA	SIGNATURE TUNE UP TO END.
	(Applause)
MAX & ORCHESTRA	'CRAZY RHYTHM' PLAYOUT.

THE MIGHTY WURLITZER

The Goon Show: No. 140 (6th Series, No. 15)
Transmission: Tuesday, 27th December 1955:
8.30—9.00 p.m. Home Service
Studio: The Camden Theatre, London

The main characters

Eccles	Spike Milligan
Ned Seagoon	Harry Secombe
Grytpype-Thynne	Peter Sellers
Moriarty	Spike Milligan
Major Denis Bloodnok	Peter Sellers
Miss Minnie Bannister	Spike Milligan
Mr Henry Crun	Peter Sellers
Bluebottle	Peter Sellers

The Ray Ellington Quartet
Max Geldray
Orchestra Conducted by Wally Stott
Announcer: Wallace Greenslade
Script by Spike Milligan
Production by Peter Eton

Young Ned Seagoon, driven by a driving ambition to become the world's greatest organ player, leaves his native Wales in order to pursue his musical studies in the Sahara. There, racing across the sands in the cockpit of his 50-ton brass-bound Wurlitzer, Ned meets unscrupulous villains Grytpype-Thynne and Count Moriarty, scrapdealers by appointment and pur-chasers of arms for Egypt. They have other plans for the Mighty Wurlitzer, however, which lead Neddie to a hair-raising race on Dayton Beach against ace organ pilots Crun and Bannister, in a desperate attempt to beat the land speed record for Wurlitzers. But it is a different record that poor Neddie breaks...

BILL	This is the BBC Home Service. Hip. Hip.
ORCHESTRA & CAST	*(crisp)* Hooray.
BILL	Oh, what fun we are having. Listeners will excuse this breach of Corporation discipline, but, well — it is the festive season so — whoopee! *(Finger in mouth wobble)*
HARRY	Mr. Greenslade! Stop taking those naughty elderly men's get fit hormones.
BILL	Get knotted, little Welsh bum.
HARRY	What what what what what? Have a care, large bloated-type announcing gentleman or I'll belt the back of that great fat greasy nut of yours.
BILL	Don't speak to me in those severe overtones. I'll have you know that I've been very ill. In fact I was at death's door twice.
HARRY	*(dry)* Why didn't you knock. Enough of this Noel Coward-type dialogue. Remove those stained-glass corsets and give the listening listeners the old posh wireless chat there.
BILL	Ladies and gentlemen, presenting the extraordinary talking-type wireless Goon Show.
HARRY	Hip Hip.
SPIKE	*(Raspberry)*
HARRY	Ta. Tonight's play was written by that great homeless author Lucky 'Smiling Jim' Milligan, now living in a damp leather bucaine off the coast of Highgate.
SPIKE	Oooooooh yes. Tonight I present my masterpiece entitled — ohh — 'The Mighty Wurlitzer'. Oooo.
ORCHESTRA	CRASHING DESCENDING CHORDS.
GRAMS	ORGAN PLAYING BACH'S TOCATA AND FUGUE.
SPIKE	*(acid)* Hear that sound, listeners? Ha ha.
SEAGOON	Yes, we can all hear it — Bach's Tocata and Fugue — by Batch. Written especially for Reg Dixon and his Blackpool Tower. It was that music that meed up my mooned to tik up the organ — but that started many years ago in the Rhonda Valley back.
ORCHESTRA	'SOSPAN BACH' MOTIF.
F.X.	VERY HEAVY DOOR RATTLING — DOOR OPENS.
SPIKE	Hear that sound listeners? A door.
SEAGOON	*(coming in)* Sospach Bach an ...
PETER	*(Mai Jones)* Who's that?
SEAGOON	I just brought your saucepan bach. Ha ha ha.
PETER	Oh, it's Neddie son bach back from the pit bach. You're back from the pit early bach?

SEAGOON	Yes — I found a piece of coal so they sent me home.
PETER	Oh lovely. Now sit down on grandad and eat your nice reeking black bread and goat pie bach.
SEAGOON	You killed the goat for Christmas bach?
PETER	We had to — he ate the turkey, only way we could get it back bach.
SPIKE	Meiouw.
SEAGOON	Puss, puss, come here, puss bach.
SPIKE	Meiouw, meiouw bach.
SEAGOON	*(dry)* That's the first time I've heard a cat bark.
F.X.	**DOOR OPENS. GALLOPING COCONUT SHELLS FAST.**
ECCLES	Hello, Neddie bach.
SEAGOON	Oh, it's Eccles, the looney.
ECCLES	Hello Nedieee — hello Nedieeee.
SEAGOON	What the hell are you talking about?
ECCLES	I've been taking talking lessons — I'm going ter be an actor. To be or not to be, Neddie.
SEAGOON	Shakespeare, eh?
ECCLES	No, dat was Hamlet.
SEAGOON	Have you seen Richard the Third?
ECCLES	No — he died before I was born.
SEAGOON	Dead? He can't be — why, only last week I saw him in a film.
ECCLES	Must have been an old one. Friends, Romans and countrymen — lend me your ears. I come to ....
SEAGOON	Shut up, Eccles.
ECCLES	Shut up, Eccles.
PETER	Neddie, what's this I hear? You playing the organ in the chapel?
SEAGOON	Oh yes, mother — play it lovely I do.
PETER	Oh, then why have half the congregation changed their religion?
SEAGOON	They don't appreciate a musical genius. You'll see, one day I'll be another Reg the Dixon — another Sandy the MacNabs.
F.X.	**HEAVY DOOR KNOB RATTLING. DOOR OPENS.**
SPIKE	Hear that sound, listeners? A door.
BILL	*(English)* Good evening, Mrs. Seagoon bach. Look you, 'tis I, isn't it bach.
SEAGOON	*(dry)* Who're you kidding?

PETER	It's Greenslade the talker — lovely man he is too. Pull up Eccles and sit down.
ECCLES	Ohhhhhh.
BILL	Sorry, bach. Mrs. Seagoon, may I see you alone?
PETER	Ohhh, you devil, and my husband still in the house too.
BILL	Madam, I came here merely to discuss Neddie. The villagers have sent me here with this money to send Neddie away for a musical education. *(Goes off talking)* We realise that he has . . . .
SEAGOON	And so Eccles and I left the village — as we reached the top of the hill we turned and waved and the villagers replied.
GRAMS	**RIFLE SHOTS. RICOCHETS IN FOREGROUND.**
SPIKE	Hear that sound, dear listeners? Ha ha.

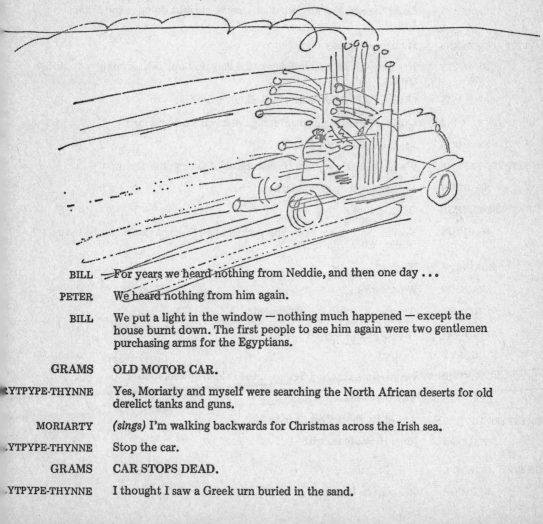

BILL	For years we heard nothing from Neddie, and then one day . . .
PETER	We heard nothing from him again.
BILL	We put a light in the window — nothing much happened — except the house burnt down. The first people to see him again were two gentlemen purchasing arms for the Egyptians.
GRAMS	**OLD MOTOR CAR.**
YTPYPE-THYNNE	Yes, Moriarty and myself were searching the North African deserts for old derelict tanks and guns.
MORIARTY	*(sings)* I'm walking backwards for Christmas across the Irish sea.
YTPYPE-THYNNE	Stop the car.
GRAMS	**CAR STOPS DEAD.**
YTPYPE-THYNNE	I thought I saw a Greek urn buried in the sand.

MORIARTY	What's a Greek earn?
GRYTPYPE-THYNNE	It's a vase made by Greeks for carrying liquids.
MORIARTY	I didn't expect that answer.
GRYTPYPE-THYNNE	Neither did quite a few smart alec listeners. Drive on — wait — listen.
GRAMS	THE ORGAN APPROACHING AT SPEED — AND PASSES.
SPIKE	Hear that sound, listeners?
MORIARTY	By the great bursting sweaters of Sabrina — did you see that?
GRYTPYPE-THYNNE	Gad, yes — a man driving a cinema organ at speed.
MORIARTY	I can't understand it, the nearest Odeon is at Clapham.
GRYTPYPE-THYNNE	Then the poor devil's lost.
MORIARTY	Lost? Sapristi Noblers, what's a cinema organist doing in the Sahara Desert?
GRYTPYPE-THYNNE	It might be Sandy on holiday.
MORIARTY	It's always Sandy on holiday in the Sahara. Look, he's turning round. He's coming back.
GRAMS	ORGAN APPROACHES AND SLOWS DOWN.
GRYTPYPE-THYNNE	Quick, Moriarty, put on evening dress — it's a white man.
SEAGOON	I say — hello there.
GRYTPYPE-THYNNE	We say hello there, too. Have a statue of George the Third.
SEAGOON	No thanks, they give me a headache.
GRYTPYPE-THYNNE	Oh, bad luck.
SEAGOON	Needle nardle noo. I saw you parked here, thought you might be having trouble with your car.
MORIARTY	We are.
SEAGOON	What's wrong?
MORIARTY	We can't keep up the instalments.
SEAGOON	When did you buy it?
MORIARTY	Yesterday.
GRYTPYFE-THYNNE	I say, aren't you Ned Seagoon, the golden-voiced coon?
SEAGOON	Yes, that's me.
GRYTPYPE-THYNNE	At last we meet then, face to face.
SEAGOON	(dry) Horrible isn't it?
GRYTPYPE-THYNNE	Only for me.
SEAGOON	Remains to be seen.

GRYTPYPE-THYNNE	What?
SEAGOON	A turkey after Christmas. Ha ha.
SPIKE	*(quick)* Hear that joke, dear listeners?
GRYTPYPE-THYNNE	Man to man, Neddie, how's the record selling?
SEAGOON	It's number scrimpson scree and throo on Housewives' Choice and third on —
MORIARTY	Stop this crazy-type talking — let's get going, Grytpype. My wife is waiting for you to come home.

GRYTPYPE-THYNNE	Not so fast, crazy-type frog-eater. Neddie? Allow me to introduce my heavily-oiled friend, Count Fred Moriarty, crack leather bucaine player and voted Mr. Thin Legs of 1912.
MORIARTY	Correction, Thin Leg.
GRYTPYPE-THYNNE	Leg?
MORIARTY	Yes, I only entered one. Now Seagoon — tell us, what is that fifty-ton brass-bound contraption you're driving?
SEAGOON	It's a Wurlitzer.
MORIARTY	We thought it was a mirage.
SEAGOON	A mirage? I've never heard of that make. Ha ha.
GRYTPYPE-THYNNE	Gad, what wit. You're not the famous Evelyn Waugh, are you?
SEAGOON	Heavens no, I wasn't born till 1918.
GRYTPYPE-THYNNE	Then you must be the famous 1918 Waugh.
SEAGOON	Needle nardle noo.
GRYTPYPE THYNNE	Touché.
SEAGOON	Threeché.
MORIARTY	Sabrina.
OMNES	*(sharp)* Hooray.
GRYTPYPE-THYNNE	Glad we all agree. While the listeners are wondering what this all means — here is Max Geldray to pay his perforated Arabian neck twig and steam boot.
MAX & ORCHESTRA	'I'M IN THE MOOD FOR LOVE'.
	(Applause)

BILL	The Mighty Wurlitzer, Part Two, hip hip.
OMNES	Hooray.
BILL	Ta. It did not take long for Grytpype-Thynne to realise that Neddie's mighty high-speed organ would make good gun barrels for the tanks now waiting at Antwerp for shipment to Egypt.
SEAGOON	They took me to lunch at the swank Hotel des Wogs in Cairo.
GRAMS	WOG TRIO.
RYTPYPE-THYNNE	Ahh, enjoy the meal, Neddie?
SEAGOON	Burp.
RYTPYPE-THYNNE	Splendid.
SEAGOON	You ask me why I only play my organ whilst travelling at speed — or faster — well, I didn't want people to copy my technique — didn't like them looking over my shoulder — so the answer was, keep moving.
MORIARTY	You are brilliant — the cleverest idiot I have met.
SEAGOON	Then you haven't met the man who pumps the organ — Eccles?
F.X.	FAST COCONUT SHELLS.
ECCLES	Hello, Neddie. Now is the winter of our discontent —
SEAGOON	Shut up, Eccles.
ECCLES	Shut, up, Eccles.
SEAGOON	Shut up.
ECCLES	Shut up.

GRYTPYPE-THYNNE	Sit down, Mr. Eccles. Now you're here you can do something useful.
ECCLES	What?
GRYTPYPE-THYNNE	Go away. No, better still, put this to your head and pull the trigger.
F.X.	PISTOL SHOT.
ECCLES	Ooooooooh ooooooooh oooooh oooh ooooo.
GRYTPYPE-THYNNE	Thank you. Now Neddie, I suppose you're wondering why we brought you here.
SEAGOON	I've been wondering why you brought me here.
GRYTPYPE-THYNNE	Neddie, we've heard you play the organ and we don't think you have it.
SEAGOON	Rubbish. Next to Reg Dixon I'm the greatest player in the world.
MORIARTY	Nonsense, Ena Baga could play better than you.
SEAGOON	I'd like to hear Ena Baga try it.
MORIARTY	Little tone-deaf lad, I am an authority on organ playing. You haven't a hope of becoming a great player.

SEAGOON	What! *(Sobs)* Oh, what a terrible turrible shock, ten years I've studied organ playing in the Sahara and now — failure — I ask you — what can I do with my fifty-ton brass-bound organ?
GRYTPYPE-THYNNE	May I make a suggestion?
SEAGOON	*(suspicious)* What?
GRYTPYPE-THYNNE	You could be the first man to break the world's land speed record in a Wurlitzer.
SEAGOON	I've never heard such a ridiculous idea.
GRYTPYPE-THYNNE	Neither have I, but there it is.
MORIARTY	Neddie, if you did this thing, it would make Reg Dixon green with envy.
SEAGOON	Mmm, that sounds interesting. What do you say, Eccles?
ECCLES	Nuttin', I'm dead.
SEAGOON	And it suits you.
F.X.	PISTOL.
ECCLES	It suits you too.
GRYTPYPE-THYNNE	Stop this crazy-type humour. Answer, do you want to break the land speed record in a Wurlitzer?
SEAGOON	Alright, what have I to lose?
MORIARTY	Good work, Grytpype, we've got him. Ha ha ha.
BOTH	April in Paris.

ORCHESTRA	LINK MUSIC.
SEAGOON	By raising an overdraft at the Bank of Jerusalem (no mean feat in itself), I shipped my organ and its crew to Dayton beach, America, for the record run. There we engaged the world's greatest military organ engineer.
ORCHESTRA	BLOODNOK THEME.

BLOODNOK	Aeiough bleioughhh sluddd. Blangee oeioughhh — ahh, that's better.
MORIARTY	Don't come near me. *(Plot, whisper)* Bloodnok, remember, loosen all the nuts and bolts so that when he is travelling at speed the whole organ falls to pieces.
BLOODNOK	Thank you for telling me the plot. Now, what about the moolah?
MORIARTY	No money until the sabotage is done.
BLOODNOK	What?? Great steaming heaps of green splat. *(Chicken clucking noise)*
MORIARTY	Stop using that foul language.
SEAGOON	Hello, I presume you're Major Bloodnok come to help me maintain my organ.
BLOODNOK	I am — and how is the Wurlitzer this morning?
SEAGOON	Running like a bird. *(Clucking)* I warmed her up with Handel's Largo — then two laps with Reg Dixon's Blackpool Nights Medley.
BLOODNOK	What melody are you playing for the record run?
SEAGOON	Twelfth Street Rag — it's the fastest tune in the world.
BLOODNOK	Well, to wish you luck I'll have a nip of brandy. Are you going to have a tiny tot?
SEAGOON	*(dry)* If I did it would be the sensation of the medical world.
BLOODNOK	Oh, you naughty-type Wurlitzer player you!
SEAGOON	Major, I want you to meet my organ pumper, Eccles.
ECCLES	Hello, Major.
BLOODNOK	Eccles, Private Eccles — gad — me old batman — remember me, Major Bloodnok?
ECCLES	I remember you, you're Major Bloodnok. Ha ha.
BLOODNOK	Aeiough. Do you remember the good times we had?
ECCLES	I remember the good times we had.
BLOODNOK	Remember that Naafi bird?
ECCLES	I remember that Naafi bird.
BLOODNOK	What was her name — Filthy Gladys?
ECCLES	Her name was Filthy Gladys.
BLOODNOK	Oh, you were too young to enjoy it — oh, me and the lads had a wonderful time with her.
ECCLES	Yer, you and the lads had a wonderful time wid her.
BLOODNOK	Yes; oh, I wonder what became of old Filthy Gladys.
ECCLES	I married her — and deserted.
BLOODNOK	Deserted? Then why are you wearing that military medal?

ECCLES	All my clothes are at the laundry.
BLOODNOK	Heavens, you mean they accepted them?
ECCLES	Only for burning.
SEAGOON	Ha ha — all was set, then. Tomorrow, the world's land speed record for Wurlitzers — in the meantime, Ray Ellington will play his canvas porridge bin and oiled groin brush.
ORCHESTRA & CAST	Hooray.
QUARTET	MUSIC.
	(Applause)

BILL	The Mighty Wurlitzer, Part the Three. Hip hip.
OMNES	Hooray.
BILL	Ta. Next morning on Dayton beach a shock was in store for Neddie.
	(Pause)
F.X.	TAPPING AND FILING. MIN SINGS.
BILL	A second great organ was being prepared for an attack on the land speed record.
MINNIE	Bim bom biddle — skiddle skool — I'm walking backwards for Christmas across the —
CRUN	Min, Min — stop that sinful sex-crazy American-type modern rhythm singing.
MINNIE	Ahh, you're corny, Henry — remember what Jim Davidson said — get modern in six weeks or get out. Bim bom biddle — have you ever heard two love birds talk?

CRUN	Stop it, Min — you're driving me into a frenzy of evil dancing.
MINNIE	No, I'm not going to stop.
BOTH	*(Argue)*
	STOP
BOTH	*(Argue)*
	STOP
BOTH	*(Argue)*
	STOP
CRUN	*(hysteria)* Stop it — ahhhh — stop that crazy rhythm, you sinful woman Min — stop it. *(Vapours)* Aahhhhh — oooooh — now let's get on with the work. Have you cleared that E flat pipe yet?
MINNIE	Yes buddy — try it.
GRAMS	**ONE OR TWO TOOTS ON ORGAN.**
SPIKE	Hear that sound, listeners — huh?
CRUN	Eureka! It's clear, Min — it sounds real cool. Get your woollen crash helmet on — I'm taking it out on the trial run.
MINNIE	You're taking my crash helmet on a trial?
CRUN	No, no, Min. Now get in, buddy — hold tight.
GRAMS	**MOTOR CAR STARTING. PROGRESSION OF GEAR CHANGING INTO DIFFERENT SPEED TUNES (GOES INTO DISTANCE WITH MINNIE SINGING).**
SEAGOON	Great wrinkled things: Did you see that, Moriarty?
MORIARTY	Yes, I saw that, Moriarty.
SEAGOON	Another organ trying to break the record. This is more than fat and bone can stand. Any of you spectators have any knowledge of that organ?
BLUEBOTTLE	Yes — I have certain knowledges. Enter Bluebottle.
SEAGOON	Ah, here is a little cardboard East Finchley mechanic.
BLUEBOTTLE	Yes.
SEAGOON	Lad lad lad, tell me, what speed does Mr. Crun's organ do?
BLUEBOTTLE	No, I shall not telle-d, I have been sworn to secrecy by Mr. Crunge.
SEAGOON	Lad lad lad, tell me, and these two ounces of cardboard brandy balls are yours.
BLUEBOTTLE	Coo, brandy balls. Thinks, with those-type sweets my prestige will increase at school. Eh, thinks again, if I gave one of them to Winnie Hemp, it might act like a love philtre on her. And then — o ehhhh ehhhh.
SEAGOON	Thinks. You dirty little devil.

COMPTON ORGAN

FIR BRIGA

BLUEBOTTLE	Thinks. Are you referring to me?
SEAGOON	Thinks. Yes I am.
BLUEBOTTLE	Thinks. You big fat steaming nit you.
SEAGOON	Thinks. Take that.
F.X.	WALLOP. TRY A FLAT NEWSPAPER ON A WOOD BOARD.
BLUEBOTTLE	Thinks. Oooooooohhhhhhh.
SEAGOON	There, there, don't take it so hard — it was only in thinks.
BLUEBOTTLE	Mmm, thinks — doesn't say anything — just thinks.
SEAGOON	Here, lad — here are the brandy balls — how fast does Mr. Crun's Wurlitzer go?
BLUEBOTTLE	Eighty mumph.
SEAGOON	Mumph?
BLUEBOTTLE	Yes. M.P.H. Mumph.
SEAGOON	Gad. Gid. Mine's only ever done 50 mphs!
MORIARTY	It *must* be destroyed! (This means more scrap for us, listeners.) Here, Ned, put this bomb in their E flat organ pipe.
SEAGOON	I'm too fat to get in that.
MORIARTY	Let's see now, who's thin enough . . . Mmm —
BLUEBOTTLE	Can I go home now, capatain, I got my . . .
SEAGOON	Yes you . . .
GRAMS	WHOOSH AWAY.
BLUEBOTTLE	(*miles away*) Goodbye.
SEAGOON	Bluebottle, come down off that Mount Everest.
BLUEBOTTLE	(*miles off — affrighted*) No no no — you will dead me — 'blange' you will go, and I will be blanged.
SEAGOON	Here's a picture of Sabrina.
GRAMS	WHOOSH.
BLOODNOK	Where where???
SEAGOON	Ah, Bloodnok, you'll do. Put this bomb in Crun's Wurlitzer.
BLOODNOK	What? I'll do it, but for fifty pounds.
SEAGOON	Gad. There are no flies on you.
BLOODNOK	I know, but they'll be back in the spring.
SEAGOON	There — fifty pounds in used custard.

F.X.	TILL.
BLOODNOK	Oh, the old Jewish piano. Aeioughh.
GRAMS	CRUN'S ORGAN DRIVES UP TO A STOP.
MINNIE	Ahh — we've just done sixty miles an hour, buddy.
SEAGOON	I'll beat that. Stand aside. So saying, I sprang into the cockpit of my Wurlitzer.
GRAMS	ORGAN STARTS UP — THEN FALLS TO PIECES. SOUND OF GREAT HOLLOW ORGAN PIPES HITTING THE CONCRETE PAVEMENTS.
MORIARTY	Hoee arr, good work, Bloodnok.
SEAGOON	*(approach)* Oohh oh, cruel, cruel fate. My Wurlitzer — fallen to pieces.
CRUN	Then we hold the record for Wurlitzers. Whooppeee!
SEAGOON	No, I'll not be forestalled or fivestalled — out of my way.
BLOODNOK	So saying, he sprang into Crun's Wurlitzer and strapped himself to the playing seat.
GRAMS	STARTS UP. DRIVES AWAY.
MORIARTY	Did you put the bomb in?
BLOODNOK	Er, let me think . . .

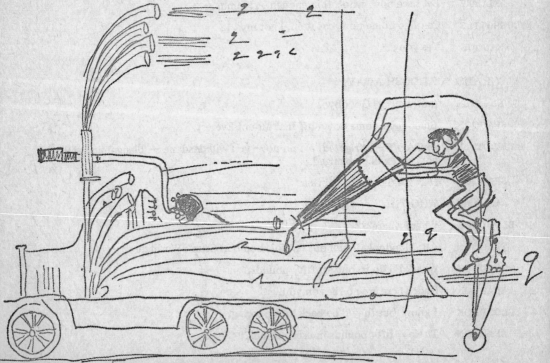

GRAMS	EXPLOSION.
BILL	And that, ladies and gentlemen, was how Neddie Seagoon broke the world altitude record for organs.
BLUEBOTTLE	*(off)* Can I come down off this Mount Everest now?
BILL	Yes yes. That was The Goon Show — a BBC recorded programme featuring Peter Sellers, Harry Secombe and Spike Milligan with the Ray Ellington Quartet and Max Geldray. The orchestra was conducted by Wally Stott. Script by Spike Milligan. Announcer: Wallace Greenslade. The programme was produced by Peter Eton.
BLUEBOTTLE	*(Echoes all the announcements)*
BILL	*(after all announcements)* For heaven's sake, shut up.
BLUEBOTTLE	For heaven's sake, shut up.
BILL	Look, if you don't stop ruining my announcing I'll —
BLUEBOTTLE	Don't you hit me — I'll tell my dad.
BILL	You do and I'll tell my mother.
	(Fade on terrific argument)
	(Applause)
MAX & ORCHESTRA	'CRAZY RHYTHM' PLAYOUT.

THE HASTINGS FLYER

The Goon Show: No. 141 (6th Series, No. 16)
Transmission: Tuesday, 3rd January 1956:
8.30—9.00 p.m. Home Service
Studio: The Camden Theatre, London

The main characters

Eccles	Spike Milligan
Ned Seagoon	Harry Secombe
Grytpype-Thynne	Peter Sellers
Moriarty	Spike Milligan
Major Denis Bloodnok	Peter Sellers
Miss Minnie Bannister	Spike Milligan
Mr Henry Crun	Peter Sellers
Bluebottle	Peter Sellers

The Ray Ellington Quartet
Max Geldray
Orchestra Conducted by Wally Stott
Announcer: Wallace Greenslade
Script by Spike Milligan
Production by Peter Eton

Our story begins on the night of the Great English Blizzard. Owing to a severe outbreak of hand-tying on his snow-plough, Neddie Seagoon, engine driver extraordinary, has been foiled in his valiant attempt to clear the line between Hastings and Pevensey Bay for the Hastings Flyer. His hi-jacked snow-plough races on through the night – at the wheel, two unscrupulous down and out MPs with a dastardly plan to wreck the Flyer. Things look pretty hopeless for Neddie as he lies bound hand and foot in a snow-drift. Meanwhile, midnight ticks nearer and nearer ... The Flyer, unaware of its danger, thunders on towards Pevensey Bay ... And in a signal box west of Pevensey Bay station, the crime of the century is about to be committed ...

BILL	This is the BBC Home Service. I would like to —
GRAMS	SHORT SHARP TRAIN WHISTLE. TRAIN CHUGS OFF AT CARTOON SPEED.
HARRY	Well that got rid of him. In the meantime here is — THEGS!! Yes, THEGS. That's the short way of saying the Highly Esteemed Goon Show. THEGS!!!
GRAMS	SOLO CHINESEWOMAN SINGING HIGH-PITCHED WAILING SONG — SPEED IT UP TO GET A HIGH VIBRATO.
PETER	Gad — how Our Gracie has changed.
SPIKE	Yes — I tell you that Isle of Capri is a sinful place.
HARRY	Silence, Tom.
SPIKE	Sorry, Dick.
PETER	I should think so too, Jim.
HARRY	Don't interrupt, Ned. Rest your head on this razor blade and listen to the story of 'The Hastings Flyer — Robbed'.
ORCHESTRA	GREAT BUILDING TYMPANY ROLL. ANTI-CLIMAXED BY ppppppp demi-semi-quaver chord.
HARRY	Thank you. Here to open the tale of the great drama is Poet and Tragedian — William J. MacGoonagle.
ORCHESTRA	MACGOONAGLE THEME (PLAYED VERY SOFTLY).
PETER	Oooooooo — 'Twas in the month of December In the year of eighteen eighty-two The railways lines near Pevensey Bay Were buried under the snoo.
ECCLES	Ooo.
PETER	All thro' the night the blizzard fiend Did like a lion roar, The snow rose up from inches three To inches three foot four . . . And ooooo the snowwww . . . .
GRAMS	WIND UP AND OUT.
SEAGOON	My name is Neddie Seagoon, engine driver extraordinary. On the night of the great English blizzard I was dragged from a warm seat in Leicester Square and taken before the director of the famed Filthmuck and Scrampson Railway.
LEW	Nedddie — little tittle Neddie, sit down — here, have a chopped liver cigarette.
SEAGOON	No thanks, I always chop my own.

LEW	Good luck. Listen, Schlapper — the line between Hastings and Pevensey Bay station is under twenty feet of Schnow. Neddie, we want you to drive a snow-plough and clear the line before midnight.
SEAGOON	But that would be a dangerous task.
LEW	It isss, it isss.
SEAGOON	I'll do it.
LEW	Good Schlapper — here's a kosher wine gum. Off you go.
SEAGOON	Oh — thanks very much.
F.X.	DOOR CLOSES.

SEAGOON	My duty was clear — clear the line at Pevensey Bay before midnight leaving it clear for the Hastings Flyer to come through. Having given the listeners the plot, I made my way towards Euston Station.
MORIARTY	Pardon me, little low suit-type man.
SEAGOON	The stranger had stepped out of a dark overcoat — another man stood on his shoulders.
GRYTPYPE-THYNNE	Have you a match?
SEAGOON	Only my own private one.
GRYTPYPE-THYNNE	Don't look so worried, my friend and I here are only MPs.
SEAGOON	If you're politicians, why are you begging in the gutter?
GRYTPYPE-THYNNE	Liberals.
SEAGOON	I understand. Can I help?

MORIARTY	Are you walking Euston station way?
SEAGOON	Yes.
MORIARTY	Could you give us a lift?
SEAGOON	I've just had my dinner.
MORIARTY	Then you're full up.
SEAGOON	Needle nardle noo.
GRYTPYPE-THYNNE	Any room in the boot?
SEAGOON	Sorry, there's a foot in it.
GRYTPYPE-THYNNE	Curse, we'll have to run alongside you.
SEAGOON	I'll go slow.
GRYTPYPE-THYNNE	Thank you, Nurke — have a gorilla.
SEAGOON	No thanks — this street is non-smoker.
GRYTPYPE-THYNNE	I see. Neddie — my heavily-oiled friend here and I are anxious to get to Pevensey Bay station tonight.
SEAGOON	You'll never do it — there are no trains.
GRYTPYPE-THYNNE	We know — perhaps a lift on your snow-plough?
SEAGOON	Out of the question — it's against the rules.
GRYTPYPE-THYNNE	We have money.
SEAGOON	Money?
GRYTPYPE-THYNNE	Yes, to prove we're not lying, here's a photograph of a shilling.
SEAGOON	*(gasp)* What wealth.
GRYTPYPE-THYNNE	And there are more photographs where that came from.
SEAGOON	*(aside)* Gad, with that treasure horde I could buy another match!!! No! I will not be tempted.
GRYTPYPE-THYNNE	Very well, Moriarty? Plan two — I'll play the violin.
ORCHESTRA	VIOLIN — 'HEARTS AND FLOWERS'.
MORIARTY	Neddie, have a heart, lad — we must get to Pevensey Bay tonight. You see, Neddie, at midnight the Hastings Flyer is coming through — all we want to do is hold it up, blow open the mail van and take the gold bullion inside. Ohhh.
SEAGOON	Stop. You're breaking my heart — I cannot refuse so simple a request — be at platform three in ten minutes or platform ten in three minutes, whichever suits you best — but remember — bring me my photographs of the money.
ORCHESTRA	MACGOONAGLE THEME.

PETER	Oooooooo Thro' the night the blizzard raged It covered Pevensey Bay station Inside the ticket office there The staff were in charge of the situation. Ooooo.
GRAMS	WIND.
MINNIE	Bim bom biddle deee bim bom I do dee —
CRUN	Min? What's the — stop that sinful singing —
MINNIE	It's the modern-style singing, buddy.
CRUN	I'm not interested in the modern style, Min — I'm more worried why we haven't sold any tickets today.
MINNIE	I can't understand it.
CRUN	Neither can I — it's the peak of our winter tourists' season.
MINNIE	Mmm — what's the weather like out?
CRUN	I can't see for all this snow coming down.
MINNIE	I think we'd better lock up for the night, Hen.
CRUN	Yes — only an idiot would come out on a night like this.
F.X.	KNOCK. KNOCK. KNOCK.
CRUN	Ohhh —
F.X.	DOOR OPENS — GALE — WIND UP.
ECCLES	Hellooooo. I'm the famous Eccles.

CRUN	Oh.
ECCLES	Well, I better be getting along now. Good day.
CRUN	Goodnight.
F.X.	**DOOR CLOSES. WIND DOWN.**
CRUN	What a nice man to come a-visiting on such a night.
MINNIE	Very nice.
CRUN	Did you see that lovely brown paper suit he was wearing?
MINNIE	I did, Henery — there's lots of money about these days.
CRUN	Ahh. Well off to bed you go, Min — I'll keep the ticket office open a little longer just in case there's a sudden rush from the Continent.
MINNIE	Ooo — I think we . . . *(Fading self off)*.
GRAMS	**WINDS UP AND UNDER:—**
PETER	Oooooooo And thro' the night, the snow-plough train Was racing down the line A lonely spectator who saw it pass Looked up and said —
ECCLES	Fine, fine.
PETER	Ooooo —
GRAMS	**OLD TRAIN CHUGGING ALONG. FADE UNDER:—**
SEAGOON	Gad — race on, steel juggernaut — it's a wonder men can live at this speed.

GRYTPYPE-THYNNE	Can't we go any faster?
SEAGOON	Faster? Ha ha — you mad fool, we're doing eight miles an hour now.
GRYTPYPE-THYNNE	Come on — be a devil.
SEAGOON	Right. Ellington? Take another twig out of the safe and hurl it on the furnace.
RAY	Needle nardle noo.
SEAGOON	Well said — now, what's the steam boiler pressure?
RAY	Ninety-eight degrees.
SEAGOON	Right — run my bath.
MORIARTY	Don't be a fool — this is no time to take a bath, it's getting late.
SEAGOON	Nonsense — plenty of time — according to the hairs on my wrist it's only half past ten.
GRYTPYPE-THYNNE	(disbelief) The hairs on your wrist say half past ten?
SEAGOON	Yes.
GRYTPYPE-THYNNE	You must be mad.
SEAGOON	Why?
GRYTPYPE-THYNNE	The hairs on my wrist say eleven-thirty.
MORIARTY	Yes, he set them by the hairs on Big Ben.
SEAGOON	Still time for a bath *and* Max Geldray!
MAX & ORCHESTRA	'ONE TWO BUTTON MY SHOE'
	(Applause)
ORCHESTRA	RETURN TO STORY LINK.
GRAMS	TRAIN CHUGGING THROUGH THE DRIVING BLIZZARD.
SEAGOON	As I sat having my bath in the back of the snow-plough — a foul trick was played.
GRYTPYPE-THYNNE	Hands up, Neddie. Moriarty, tie his hands — then hide them where he can't find them.
SEAGOON	What a fiendish move — you naughty men — I'll write to *The Times* about this —
F.X.	FURIOUS PEN SCRATCHING ON VELLUM OR PAPER.
SEAGOON	Dear Sir — I wish to complain about an outbreak of hand-tying on snow-ploughs whilst taking hip baths.
GRYTPYPE-THYNNE	(furious) Give me that letter — you'll not send that, lad — now ....
F.X.	FURIOUS WRITING.

YTPYPE-THYNNE	Dear sir — today I heard the first cuckoo — there, sign that —
F.X.	PEN.
YTPYPE-THYNNE	Good — Moriarty, post it — that'll put them off the track.
MORIARTY	I'll just tie his hands again — ahhh — there.
YTPYPE-THYNNE	Good — now cut the knot off so he can't untie it.
MORIARTY	Right — here — put it in your pocket. Now, together — one! two!
SEAGOON	No, don't throw me out.
MORIARTY	Three.
SEAGOON	Helllll (going off) pppppppp —
GRAMS	UPWARD RUSH OF TRAIN — STEAM — ROAR OF THE WHEELS GOING INTO DISTANCE (PAUSE) THEN JUST THE HOWL OF THE BLIZZARD.
SEAGOON	I lay gasping on the railway bank — with the knot of my bonds in Grytpype-Thynne's pocket — it looked pretty hopeless for me —
ORCHESTRA	(APPROACHING) BIG DRUM BEATING IN MARCH TIME.
BLOODNOK	Ooo — I say — have you seen a band go this way?
SEAGOON	No, I'm sorry, I've only just arrived here.
BLOODNOK	Oh, I must find them — they might be playing a different tune from me by now. Wait a minute — I know you — aren't you Neddie Seagoon, the singing dwarf and current number one with the Grades?
SEAGOON	If you put it that way — I am. And you, aren't you the blaggard embezzler, no-good soak and layabout, Denis Bloodnok?
BLOODNOK	If you put it that way — I am. And what are you doing here?
SEAGOON	I've just been thrown off a train.
BLOODNOK	Any decent driver would have done the same!
SEAGOON	If my hands weren't tied I'd strike you down with my mackerel pie and thunder straw.
BLOODNOK	Your hands are tied?
SEAGOON	Yes.
BLOODNOK	Ooo.
SEAGOON	Bloodnok, take your hands off my wallet!
BLOODNOK	(going off) Three pound ten — four pound, four pounds —
SEAGOON	Come back with my wallet, you — the devil, he's gone — thank heaven he didn't find my money belt.
GRAMS	APPROACHING WHOOSH.

BLOODNOK	Aeioughh.
SEAGOON	Take your hands off my money belt!
BLOODNOK	Ten *(going off fast)* eleven pound twelve — Merry Christmas. *(Goes off)*
SEAGOON	The devil — taken all the money I stole from the kiddies' bank — but time was wasting — I had to warn the approaching Hastings Flyer of the plot to wreck her. So thinking, I stumbled forwards through the blizzard — I made a pair of snow shoes but the heat of my feet melted them. Suddenly, from a nearby frozen pool I hear —
GRAMS	SPLASH. MAN SWIMMING ON BACK, KICKING LEGS.
ECCLES	*(off)* In the good old summer timeee — in the good old summer timeee —
SEAGOON	I say, you — don't you feel cold in there?
ECCLES	Nope — I got my overcoat on.
SEAGOON	Listen, I've got to get to Pevensey Bay Station as soon as possible.
ECCLES	*(on)* I'm the famous Eccles.
SEAGOON	Yes — hey! That tricycle against the wall — whose is it?
ECCLES	Mine — a present from an admirer.
SEAGOON	Could you drive me to town on it?
ECCLES	Oh, the tricycle ain't mine — the wall was the present.
SEAGOON	Well, drive me there on that —
ECCLES	Right — hold tight.
GRAMS	SERIES OF MAD SOUNDS PLAYED AT SPEED TO SOUND LIKE SOME KIND OF COMBUSTION ENGINE.
BILL	The sound you are hearing is Neddie and Eccles driving a wall at speed. We thought you ought to know. Meantime, at Pevensey Bay station.
F.X.	PHONE RINGS. PHONE OFF HOOK.
CRUN	Hello, Pevensey Bay station here.
PETER	*(Distort — gram recording: long mad unintelligible speech)*
CRUN	I'm sorry, he's not in.
F.X.	PHONE DOWN. DOOR BURSTS OPEN. BLIZZARD UP. DOOR CLOSES. BLIZZARD OUT.
SEAGOON	*(gasping)* Mr. Crun — has the snow-plough been through yet?
CRUN	No.
SEAGOON	Thank yuckakabakkas, we're still in time — first I must get these bonds untied — have you got a knot?
CRUN	Yes.

SEAGOON	Quick, glue one onto my bonds then untie them.
BILL	Listeners, as knot-glueing and untying has no audible sound we suggest you make your own — within reason, that is.
GRAMS	FRED, THE OYSTER.
SEAGOON	*(dry)* I knew someone would spoil it — but now my hands were free — now for action.
CRUN	What's all this about —
SEAGOON	Shhh, listen — what's that noise?
GRAMS	VERY OBVIOUS TRAIN PULLING UP AT STATION.
SEAGOON	It's a train!!!
GRAMS	STORMS OF APPLAUSE.
SEAGOON	Thank you, Seagoon fans, it was nothing.
CRUN	Mr. Seacrune — it's the snow-plough come to clear the line — hooray!!
SEAGOON	Shh, no, the two men on that snow-plough are train robbers! We must stop them.

CRUN	Oh, don't worry — the moment they step through that door I'll let them have it with this leather blunderbuss.
F.X.	**KNOCK ON DOOR.**
SEAGOON	*(whisper)* It's them — *(aloud)* Ahem — come in, nice men.
F.X.	**DOOR OPENS — ROAR OF BLUNDERBUSS.**
BLUEBOTTLE	You rotten swines you!!! What are you doing to Blunebontle — I was walking along collecting numbers like a happy boy train spotter when — blange — there was a blinding flash — I reeled backwards clutching my forehead — I looked down and my knees had gone and certain other vital things — you swines you!
SEAGOON	Little cross-eyed hairless pipe-cleaner — were you followed up the platform by two men?
BLUEBOTTLE	I'm not going to tell you — shooting me like that.
SEAGOON	Come, come, little two-stone Hercules — tell me if you saw two men and you can have this quarter of dolly mixture.
BLUEBOTTLE	Cor, dolly mixture — thinks — with those-type sweets I could influence certain girls at playtime — that Brenda Pugh might be another Rita Hayworth.
SEAGOON	Then you'll tell me?
BLUEBOTTLE	Yes — I saw the two nice men walking up the line towards the signal box — yes.
SEAGOON	We must stop them — but we'll pause first to hear Ray Ellington.
BLUEBOTTLE	Ooooo — smashin'.
QUARTET	'I WANT YOU TO BE MY BABY'.

(Applause)

BILL	Thank you, Ray Ellington. I'm sure you mean well — we rejoin 'The Hasting Flyer — Robbed' inside the signal box west of Pevensey Bay station. Which will play a vitally unimportant part in the story.
GRAMS	WIND.
WILLIUM	Zzzzzzz mate.
F.X.	PHONE BELL RINGS.
WILLIUM	Oh strufe cor blimestone a crow — zzzzzzz mate.
F.X.	PHONE BELL RINGS.
WILLIUM	Ow ow ow ow — wahszat mate?
F.X.	PHONE RINGS.
WILLIUM	Oh, it's the torking telephone ringing mate.
F.X.	PHONE RINGS.
WILLIUM	There it goes again mate.
F.X.	PHONE RINGS.
WILLIUM	And again — and unless I'm mistaken it's going to go —
F.X.	PHONE RINGS.
WILLIUM	— again mate.
F.X.	PHONE OFF HOOK.
WILLIUM	Hello, Pevensey Bay signal box man here mate.
SEAGOON	Listen mate, put the signals to danger — stop the Hasting Flyer.
WILLIUM	Oh — I'll do that —
F.X.	WALLOP ON HEAD.
SEAGOON	(distort) Hello, hello mate?
F.X.	PHONE IS DROPPED INTO PLACE ON HOOK.
GRYTPYPE-THYNNE	(very cold) All very nicely done, Moriarty mate. Now see, there's a bridge to the right — good, take these sticks of dynamite, place them in the centre of the span and run the wires back here. When the Hastings Flyer comes across — we press the plunger.
MORIARTY	Ha he ho har har — then the money from the bullion van — ho ho har, moolah — April in Paris.
BOTH	Thanks to a Charlie. (Fade)
	(Fade in)
F.X.	RATTLING OF PHONE HOOK.
SEAGOON	Hello, signal box — hello — he's hung up.
ECCLES	We'd better go and cut him down.

SEAGOON	You're right — Eccles, get your wall started.
BLUEBOTTLE	What about me, Captain — can't I come in the game?
SEAGOON	Yes — only an idiot would leave you behind.
ECCLES	Leave him behind.
SEAGOON	Silence, the famous Eccles.
ECCLES	Silence, the famous Eccles.
SEAGOON	Bluebottle — take this photograph of a red flag, go and stand on the bridge near the signal box — if the Hastings Flyer approaches — stop it at all costs.
BLUEBOTTLE	Oh good — I will — I will be a hero! — My picture will be in the *East Finchley Chronic* — 'Boy hero Bluebottle' — he he — thinks — that will make that Muriel Bates run after me — but I will play hard to get — 'I'm sorry Miss Bates — I am a busy boy hero — I have certain matters to attend to — I have to be photographed with Sabrina' — he he — yesss, that's what I'll say — thinks — here *(awe)* that Sabrina a fine big girl. Heee.
BLUEBOTTLE	Yes — he he — thinks — I better start wearin' long trousers soon.
MINNIE	Oh dear. Mr. Secrune — don't leave us alone with those two train robbers about — we'll be murdered in our ticket offices.
SEAGOON	Don't worry, Miss Bannister — here, take this copy of the *Nursing Mother* — if you're attacked — don't hesitate to use it.
MINNIE	Safe at last. Oooooo.
SEAGOON	My dear madam with your face you'd be safe in Portsmouth on pay night.
MINNIE	Oooo.
SEAGOON	Come men, we must hurry — the hairs on my wrist say it's quarter to needle nardle noo.
BLUEBOTTLE	Yes, forward to the bridge.
ORCHESTRA	**VERY TATTY BOYS' BRIGADE MARCH. FADE OUT.**
GRAMS	**FADE UP BLIZZARD AND DOWN.**
WILLIUM	Ow ow ow — you hit me on me head and tied me up mates.
MORIARTY	Shut up mate — Sapristi nuckoes yuk yuk kuk kuk — Grytpype — the hairs on my wrist say it's midnight o'clock — and no sign of the Hastings Flyer.
GRYTPYPE-THYNNE	Steady, frog-eater — obviously the blizzard has delayed the train.
MORIARTY	*(cracks up)* I'm not going to wait any longer — my nerves are strained to breaking point.
F.X.	**BOINGG!!**
MORIARTY	There goes one now — ohh, I can't stand the —
GRYTPYPE-THYNNE	Shut up! Open your mouth.

MORIARTY	Ahhh —
RYTPYPE-THYNNE	Close it.
GRAMS	**GRENADE EXPLODES IN MOUTH. MOUTH FULL OF TEETH FALL ON THE FLOOR.**
MORIARTY	You swine — you put a grenade in my mouth — all my choppers have gone — my teeth.
RYTPYPE-THYNNE	Yes, let that be a lesson to you — now control yourself.
GRAMS	**SOUND OF BLOODNOK BEARING HIS BASS DRUM.**
RYTPYPE-THYNNE	Great goose hooks — look, it's a military gentleman walking up the line — banging a drum.
MORIARTY	You English are so musical.
RYTPYPE-THYNNE	Yes, the woods are full of them. Now let's sit quietly and wait for the Hastings Flyer.
GRAMS	**BLIZZARD UP. THEN UNDER.**
BLUEBOTTLE	Captain, captain, look what I found in the bridge.
SEAGOON	Dynamite — thank heaven you found it.
BLUEBOTTLE	Thank you, heaven.
SEAGOON	Good. Now put it somewhere for safety.
BLUEBOTTLE	Yes — moves right — puts dreaded dynamite under signal box for safety — does not notice dreaded wires leading to plunger up in signal cabin. Thinks. I'm for the dreaded deading alright this week.
SEAGOON	Men — our two train robbers are up in that signal cabin. Eccles, you go up the line and try to stop the Hastings Flyer — I'll try and put the signals to danger.
ECCLES	O.K.
SEAGOON	Bluebottle, you keep me covered with this photograph of a gun. Right — let's go in —
F.X.	**DOOR KICKED.**
SEAGOON	Hands up!
MORIARTY	Sapristi, look: Sabrina.
SEAGOON	Wrong, it's me with my arms folded!
RYTPYPE-THYNNE	So, Neddie, you managed to get your hands free.
SEAGOON	Yes — they never cost me a penny, thanks to National Health!
GRAMS	**DISTANT TOOT OF TRAIN APPROACHING.**
MORIARTY	It's the Hastings Flyer — with all that money on board — ohh, foiled!
SEAGOON	Yes — I've got to stop it or it'll crash into the snow plough at Pevensey Bay station.

GRYTPYPE-THYNNE	*(idea)* Oh — er — you can easily stop it — just press that little plunger with the wires leading out the window.
SEAGOON	Right — ugh!
GRYTPYPE-THYNNE	*(aside)* Here goes the bridge, Mori —
GRAMS	TREMENDOUS CRACKING EXPLOSION. LITTLE BITS AND PIECES HIT THE DECK (NOT SPOT).
BLUEBOTTLE	You rotton swines, I told you I'd be deaded.
BILL	Yes, they're all deaded, but who got the money from the bullion van in the Hastings Flyer?
GRAMS	DRUMS.
ORCHESTRA	SIGNATURE TUNE: UP AND DOWN FOR:—
BILL	That was The Goon Show — a BBC recorded programme featuring Peter Sellers, Harry Secombe and Spike Milligan with the Ray Ellington Quartet and Max Geldray. The orchestra was conducted by Wally Stott. Script by Spike Milligan. Announcer: Wallace Greenslade. The programme was produced by Peter Eton.
ORCHESTRA	SIGNATURE TUNE UP TO END.
	(Applause)
MAX & ORCHESTRA	'CRAZY RHYTHM' PLAYOUT.

THE HOUSE OF TEETH

The Goon Show: No. 145 (6th Series, No. 20)
Transmission: Tuesday, 31st January 1956:
8.30—9.00 p.m. Home Service
Studio: The Camden Theatre, London

The main characters

Ned, Lord Seagoon	Harry Secombe
O'Brien (African chief)	Ray Ellington
Willium	Peter Sellers
Mr Henry Crun	Peter Sellers
Miss Minnie Bannister	Spike Milligan
Dr Londongle	Valentine Dyall
Eccles	Spike Milligan
Bluebottle	Peter Sellers
Moriarty	Spike Milligan
Grytpype-Thynne	Peter Sellers
Throat	Spike Milligan
Major Denis Bloodnok	Peter Sellers

Special Guest: Valentine Dyall ('The Man in Black')
The Ray Ellington Quartet
Max Geldray
Orchestra Conducted by Wally Stott
Announcer: Wallace Greenslade
Script by Spike Milligan
Production by Peter Eton

Who is the ghoulish Dr Londongle? And why has he a weakness for a nice smile? What was the fiendish promise made to him by sultry Signorita Gladys de la Tigernutta, queen of the castanets? Why are guests at his mysterious castle forced to become vegetarians? The surrounding peasantry live in fear until, one dark and stormy night, intrepid young Lord Seagoon, on a sight-seeing trip in his horse-drawn motor car, knocks at the dreaded castle door. Screams in the night and a trail of toothless men in brown paper nightshirts lead him to the steaming atmosphere of the notorious Café Filthmuck, where the grisly secret of the House of Teeth is finally revealed...

BILL	This is the BBC Home Service.
ECCLES	Fine fine.
BILL	Ahem. Mr. Stott! Mood music, please.
ORCHESTRA	BROODING CHORDS — NOT LOUD BUT SINISTER.
PETER	(Headstone) The jolly Goons present a play —
PETER	. . . in three parts. Part One is entitled —
GRAMS	(FAST) WALLOP ON BACK OF HEAD. POP OF LARGE POP GUN. SET OF FALSE TEETH HITTING INSIDE OF BUCKET. SCREAM. OHHHHH.
SEAGOON	I'll never forget that terrible sound, listeners — it started back in 1889 . . .
GRAMS	CRACKLE OF LIGHTNING. ROLL OF THUNDER. DRIVING RAIN. WIND SQUALLS. HORSE & CART TRUNDLING ALONG ROUGH MOUNTAIN ROAD.
SEAGOON	It was the worst storm they had ever known in the Dolomites. I, Lord Seagoon, daredevil fretwork champion, was lost with my servants on the side of a precipitous mountain in a horse-drawn motor car.
GRAMS	HORSE REARS & NEIGHS. CARRIAGE STOPS.
SEAGOON	Why have we stopped, O'Brien?
O'BRIEN	(African chief) I think the horse must be tired, sir.
SEAGOON	Why?
O'BRIEN	He's got his pyjamas on, begorrah.
WILLIUM	I think we're lost, Lord mate.
SEAGOON	Tut, tut, what a nuisance. Well, there's naught for it mate, we'll spend the night here. I'll sleep in the ditch and you sleep standing up holding an umbrella over me.
WILLIUM	I'm goin' ter vote Labour next time, mate.
SEAGOON	Silence, you political hot-head.
O'BRIEN	Lord Seagoon, me no like to spend the night on this pitch black road.
SEAGOON	Don't worry, you won't be noticed. Now, as we're staying the night here, unroll my brass bedstead and erect my marble wash stand. Abdul?
ABDUL	(approach) What you want, sahib?
SEAGOON	Before I retire prepare a light sixteen-course banquet.
ABDUL	I go and connect the gas stove up to the horse.
SEAGOON	Mind you get the right end this time. Willium? Lay out my evening dress.
WILLIUM	Cor strufe, you wearing evening dress in this rain and mud, mate?
SEAGOON	Yes — remember, all of you — we're British. Together — hip hip.

OMNES	*(miserable)* Hooray.
SEAGOON	Good. Next hoist a small Union Jack and unveil a bust of Queen Victoria. Now I'll just make a rough 'Englishman lost on the mountainside Menu'. Brown Windsor soup, meat, two veg., pots., boiled rice and jam. Fair makes your mouth water.
GRAMS	LONE BELL RINGS HIGH UP ON MOUNTAIN.
WILLIUM	Listen mate.
GRAMS	BELL.
WILLIUM	There it is again mate.
GRAMS	BELL.
WILLIUM	And again mate — 'less I'm mistaken it's going to go —
GRAMS	BELL.
WILLIUM	Again mate.
SEAGOON	What an extrasensory perception. I wonder what it is mate.
WILLIUM	It's a bell ringing mate.
SEAGOON	There you go — jumping to conclusions. We'll soon find out. O'Brien, strike one of my monogrammed matches.
F.X.	MATCH STRIKING. FLARES.
SEAGOON	Look! A castle — a mere twenty miles away. After it, before it gets away.
GRAMS	RUNNING LIKE MAD OF TEN PAIRS OF BOOTS. MEN SHOUTING — VOICES GET DISTANT AND HIGHER AS RECORD IS SPEEDED UP.
ORCHESTRA	ONE SOMBRE CHORD. WEIRD FLUTE MELODY SUPERIMPOSED.
	(Fade)
GRAMS	STORM. BUT HELD UNDER:—
SEAGOON	*(approaching)* Here we are men — this is the place.
O'BRIEN	Thank heaven — my feet have been killing me.
SEAGOON	*(dry)* You're not the only one they've been killing. Right. Abdul, hoist a French Union Jack. Now let's see how we get into this castle. Ah, a door. O'Brien, lay out my knocking-on-door suit. Now lift me up and I'll knock.
O'BRIEN	Me vote labour next time. Begorrah.
SEAGOON	Silence, O'Brien. Lift.
GRAMS	KNOCKING ON HEAVY OAK DOOR. ECHOES AWAY BEHIND ALONG THE CORRIDOR. SLOW GHOSTLY FOOTSTEPS APPROACH.
SEAGOON	Somebody's coming.

O'BRIEN	Man, I don't like this place. I'm frightened, begorrah.
SEAGOON	Silly fellow, there's nothing to be frightened of.
SPIKE	*(Echo) (Scream)*
O'BRIEN	What you say?
SEAGOON	*(miles off)* I said there's nothing to be frightened of.
O'BRIEN	Then what you doing up that tree?
SEAGOON	It makes me look taller. Apart from that I'm just unfurling a fresh Union Jack.
GRAMS	**GREAT DOOR STARTS TO OPEN WITH CHAINS, ETC.**
CRUN	Mnk — ahahaha — grmnpppp — ah.
SEAGOON	There, standing in the doorway, was a bag of dust in a night shirt. *(Aside)* Speak to him, O'Brien.
O'BRIEN	Good evening, suh.
CRUN	No coal tonight, coalman.
O'BRIEN	What????
GRAMS	**SOUND OF CRUN BEING WHIRLED AROUND A MAN'S HEAD.**

SEAGOON	O'Brien, stop swinging him round your head.
CRUN	(shaky) Ahmmmm — what's the idea?
SEAGOON	Allow me to explain.
CRUN	Explain? Eleven o'clock at night — you drag me out of bed —
SEAGOON	We couldn't have — we've been down here all the time.
CRUN	Ohhh — mnkmnnarrgg — begone or I'll strike you with this weighted piano.
SEAGOON	Not so fast, old doubled-up dada.
CRUN	(rage) I'm not a dada.
SEAGOON	(dry) Well, if you're not, it's too late now.
CRUN	(vapours) Ahhmnk, stop those sinful Sunday paper jokes.
SEAGOON	Old wrinkled retainer — listen. My retinue and I require kippo for the night — I'm willing to pay. Look, here's an advance, three shillings in unused buttons.
CRUN	Oh, I'll sew them on my cheque book at once.
SPIKE	(Echo) (Scream)
CRUN	(unruffled) Min, I think he wants to go out.
SEAGOON	(fear) Who wants to go out?
CRUN	We don't know what it is, but when it wants to go, it screams.
MINNIE	(appearing) Ohh, who are these men, Crun?
CRUN	They're men, Min — staying the night.
MINNIE	Oh, what room shall we put them in, Crun?
BOTH	(Talk very quietly about which room. They go on and on).
CRUN	Oh they've gone — where are you, sirs?
SEAGOON	(off) Upstairs in bed.

CRUN	Goodnight.
DR. LONDONGLE	Good evening, Crun. We have fresh visitors, then.
CRUN	*(a little afraid)* Ohh, Dr. Londongle.
ORCHESTRA	SOFT HORROR CHORD. TROMBONES.
CRUN	You're home early tonight, sir.
DR. LONDONGLE	Yes, Crun. It watched her dance again tonight. Oh, how she danced. *(Goes off.)*
CRUN	He's talking about Señorita la Tigernutta. Every night he goes to the Café Filthmuck to watch her dance.
DR. LONDONGLE	Yes, Crun. Three years ago she said, 'Dr. Londongle, the day you can give me fifty pairs of castanets, I'll marry you.' Well, I've got forty-eight pairs.
MINNIE	Then you only want two more pairs, eh buddy?
DR. LONDONGLE	Yes, buddy, just two. I nearly got them tonight — but just failed. Crun? Take my skull-clouting mallet and teeth-catching bucket.
SPIKE	*(Screammmm)*
DR. LONDONGLE	How sweet, the children are awake. It's little green wretch. He needs changing. See, what did I change him for last time? Ha ha ha-type laughter. Bannister — a moment of quiet meditation, play me a gramophone record.
GRAMS	SURFACE HISS. THEN WOMAN SCREAMING BEING CHASED BY A SEX-CRAZED MANIAC. GIBBERISH. LAUGHTER. THEN WALLOP. POP. CLANG OF TEETH IN BUCKET. LAST SOB THEN SILENCE.
DR. LONDONGLE	Ahh, Crun, they don't write tunes like that any more.
CRUN	Oh, Max Geldray gets pretty near it.
DR. LONDONGLE	Needle nardle noo.
MAX & ORCHESTRA	'ST. LOUIS BLUES'. *(applause)*

ORCHESTRA	THREE SOMBRE CHORDS.
PETER	Part Two — Midnight in the Castle.
GRAMS	LAST FEW STROKES OF MIDNIGHT.
O'BRIEN	*(loud)* Zzzzzzzzzzzzz.
SEAGOON	*(loud)* Zzzzzzz Zzzzzzz Zzzzzzz Zzzzzzz.
WILLIUM	You asleep mate?
SEAGOON	Of course we are. You don't think we make this noise when we're awake, do you? O'Brien, lay out my waking-up suit.
WILLIUM	*(fear)* There's something under the bed mate.
SEAGOON	Thank heaven for that.
WILLIUM	It's been moving about mate.
SEAGOON	*(dry)* I don't believe it mate.
WILLIUM	Shhhhh. Listen.
ECCLES	*(under bed) (sings)* How would you like to be — Under the bed wid me.
SEAGOON	Come out, you singer of chamber music.
ECCLES	Hellooooo.
SEAGOON	Before me stood a ragged idiot dressed in a grass skirt, water wings and a perforated bronze trilby.
ECCLES	I'm on my honeymoon.
SEAGOON	Well, where's your wife?
ECCLES	Didn't bring her.
SEAGOON	Why not?
ECCLES	Well, why should I share all the fun wid her?
SEAGOON	Get out of my room.
ECCLES	Get out of my room.
SEAGOON	Get out.
ECCLES	Get out.
F.X.	DOOR OPENS.
DR. LONDONGLE	Ahh, there you are, naughty little Eccles.
ECCLES	Hello, Doctor Londongle.
DR. LONDONGLE	Naughty lad, getting out of bed after I'd tucked you in and battered you unconscious for the night.
ECCLES	Hello, Dr. Londongle.
DR. LONDONGLE	Gentlemen, my apologies. You won't be disturbed further. *(Pause)*

SEAGOON	What are you staring at me for?
DR. LONDONGLE	What lovely teeth you have. False?
SEAGOON	No, perfectly true. They are lovely teeth. Why?
DR. LONDONGLE	*(mad)* Nothing. Goodnight.
F.X.	DOOR CLOSES.
SEAGOON	Jolly fellow. What's the time by my OBE? Gad — one o'clock. Goodnight all.
OMNES	*(fast)* Goodnight — Zzzzzzzzzzzzzz.

Fade out

Fade in

GRAMS	TWO O'CLOCK STRIKES.

OMNES	*(still)* Zzzzzzzzzzz.
DR. LONDONGLE	They're fast asleep — hand me the skull mallet. Hold the teeth bucket in front of his cake-hole. Now — ugghhh.
GRAMS	WALLOP. POP OF POP GUN. FALSE TEETH SHOOT OUT AND LAND IN BUCKET.
WILLIUM	*(no teeth)* Ohhh — mate.
SEAGOON	That was the sound I told you of earlier, dear listeners. Hurriedly I struck a match and lit a light bulb. There on the floor was Willium.
WILLIUM	Ohh, me choppers have gone mate. Someone hit me on the back of the nut and out flew my false teef.

SEAGOON	O'Brien? Lay out my looking-for-teeth suit. Willium, say 'Aaaaaahhhh'.
WILLIUM	Aaaaahhhhh.
SEAGOON	They've gone.
O'BRIEN	Wait, there's a brick on his tongue with a message tied to it.
SEAGOON	Read it.
O'BRIEN	Made by the Birmingham Brick Corporation.
SEAGOON	Not the brick, the message.
O'BRIEN	Nothing on it, begorrah.
SEAGOON	So, they won't talk, eh? Wait — I've suddenly realised something. Except for Dr. Londongle, no one else in this castle has teeth. I'm going to have a word with him. O'Brien, lay out my having-a-word-with-him suit.
F.X.	DOOR OPENS
SEAGOON	Wait here.
F.X.	DOOR SHUTS. FOOTSTEPS ALONG LONG LONELY CORRIDOR.
SEAGOON	Dr. Londongle? Dr. Loctor Donglonge — Ingledongle — Dr. . . . I want to speak to you. Dr. Longdongleeeeee.
BLUEBOTTLE	Will you stop all dat shouting! I'm trying to kip.
SEAGOON	Come here, little nurk.
BLUEBOTTLE	Here, let go my ear'ole — let go or I'll call little Jim.
SEAGOON	Call him then.
BLUEBOTTLE	Jimmm — little Jim? Jim . . .
SEAGOON	Why doesn't he answer?
BLUEBOTTLE	He's in Africa.
SEAGOON	Where's Dr. Londongle?

BLUEBOTTLE	I don't know Dister Dongler . . .
SEAGOON	Speak, rapscallion.
BLUEBOTTLE	Ohhhh — stop pulling my ear'ole. Ohh, now look what you done. You pulled it off. Give it here. I only borrowed it for the day.
SEAGOON	Come on, hairless little nurk. Who are you?
BLUEBOTTLE	I am a purehearted-type English scout on the camping-type holiday.
SEAGOON	Camping? Why are you camping indoors?
BLUEBOTTLE	It's too parky outside. I am the new type indoor scout. *(Confidentially)* Here — got any pictures of Sabrina?
SEAGOON	You dirty little devil — I'll tell your Scout Master.
BLUEBOTTLE	He's the one who told us to collect them.
SEAGOON	The naughty man — well, he won't get my collection.
BLUEBOTTLE	Can I go now? My little brownie is waiting for me.
SEAGOON	No lad — you'd better come with me. I might need you for protection. I'll use you as a club.
BLUEBOTTLE	Ehe — oh no, no, I'm no good at protection. I'm a rotten coward. Look, here's my junior coward's badge.
MORIARTY	*(off)* Ooooooo
SEAGOON	Give me that junior coward's badge. I've just qualified.
MORIARTY	*(off)* Ooooooohohoh ohohohoh ohh eheehehe hehehe oheheh.
BLUEBOTTLE	It's David Whitfield.
SEAGOON	*(dry)* Gad, he's improved.
MORIARTY	Ohhahhh.
SEAGOON	Gid gad gude. That voice is coming from under this floor. I'll just put on my floor-lifting suit. Now — lift — ugggggghhhhh. Ugghhhh — uggghhhhhhhhh.

BLUEBOTTLE	Don't stand there making a noise, give me a hand, you big fat steaming nit you.
SEAGOON	Ahem. Lift — uggghhhh.
F.X.	**STONE FLAG BEING LIFTED FROM TOP OF A DUNGEON.**
MORIARTY	*(gummy)* Ohh saved, saved — teeth — give us teeth.
OMNES	*(gummy)* Teeth teeth ohhh teethhhhhh.
SEAGOON	Dear listeners, from out of an underground dungeon came a crowd of toothless ragged men in brown paper nightshirts.
GRYTPYPE-THYNNE	*(gums)* Let me explain, short-type man. Forty-eight of us have been kept prisoner down there after having our false teeth stolen.
MORIARTY	Yes. Ohhhhhh — no teeth — we haven't eaten meat for years.
SEAGOON	Vegetarians eh? I too only eat grass-eating animals.
MORIARTY	But we must have our teeth back — ohhh.
SEAGOON	Leave it to me. First let's drop this flagstone back in place.
F.X.	**CLANG OF FLAGSTONE FALLING BACK.**
BLUEBOTTLE	Ohhhh, my foot. Look, it's shaped like a starting handle.
SEAGOON	Excellent. O'Brien? Lay out my leader-of-toothless-men suit. Right, gentlemen! Follow me. We march to find the missing teeth. One two.
OMNES	*(sing) (the Mounties' Song from 'Rose Marie')* On through the hail, like a pack of hungry wolves on the trail, we are after you, dead or alive — we are out to get you, dead or alive. *(Go off marching.)*
F.X.	**MARCHING BOX**
O'BRIEN	Folks? While I still got my choppers — here's my song, begorrah.
MINNIE	Swing it buddy.
QUARTET	**'WHO'S GOT THE MONEY'.**

(Applause)

BILL	We return you now to — Part Three. The Castle of Missing Teeth.
ORCHESTRA	DRAMATIC CHORDS.
F.X.	CASTANETS (ONE PAIR) PLAYING IN 6/8 TEMPO.
DR. LONDONGLE	Ha ha ha ha ha ha-type laughing. Aren't they beautiful, mother dear.
THROAT	Oh lovely, lovely.
DR. LONDONGLE	Another pair of castanets for Señorita La Tigernutta — that's forty-nine pairs I've got. One more pair and she's promised to be mine. So much for the tatty plot.
F.X.	KNOCK ON DOOR.
DR. LONDONGLE	Quick, mother, hide under the carpet. Come in.
F.X.	DOOR OPENS.
BLOODNOK	Oh, good evening. Any possibility of contacting the police from here?
DR. LONDONGLE	I'm afraid not.
BLOODNOK	Thank heaven, safe at last. Oeiugh.
DR. LONDONGLE	What brings you here at this late hour?
BLOODNOK	I'm lost. Me and the Regiment were marching along, when suddenly, quite by accident, me and the regimental funds took the wrong turning.
DR. LONDONGLE	How rotten for the Regiment. Don't they want you back?
BLOODNOK	Oh yes — everywhere you'll see my notices — 'Wanted — Major Bloodnok'. I shou . . . I say, why are you staring at me like that?
DR. LONDONGLE	Your teeth — are they false?
BLOODNOK	Oh yes, oh yes. What's more, they're of great sentimental value. You see *(tearful)* they belong to my great-grandmother.
DR. LONDONGLE	It must be wonderful to have a family heirloom.
BLOODNOK	Yes, do you mind if I take my kilt off, it's hot in here. Oooo!
DR. LONDONGLE	What's up?
BLOODNOK	That lump in the carpet — it moved.
DR. LONDONGLE	Yes — it's the only carpet in the world with a moving lump.
BLOODNOK	It must be valuable then.
DR. LONDONGLE	It has great sentimental value — you see *(tearful)* that lump belongs to my mother.
BLOODNOK	What a lovely heirloom to leave behind. A large lump. Oh, people aren't as thoughtful these days.
DR. LONDONGLE	This bucket you see is also an heirloom — just bend over it and look at the bottom.
BLOODNOK	I can't see anything to —

F.X.	**WALLOP. POP. CLANG.**
BLOODNOK	*(gums)* Ohh, me choppers —
DR. LONDONGLE	Got 'em. Ha ha ha ha ha.
F.X.	**DOOR BURSTS OPEN.**
SEAGOON	Not so fast, Dr. Londongler. Where are you hiding these men's teeth?
OMNES	Teeth. We want teeth.
DR. LONDONGLE	Silence — don't move, any of you, or I'll shoot.
SEAGOON	Fool — put down that tin of potted shrimps.
DR. LONDONGLE	And starve to death? Never.
SEAGOON	Londonker, I'm willing to bargain with you.
DR. LONDONGLE	What's your offer?
SEAGOON	These outsize ladies' bloomers at three and eleven three.
DR. LONDONGLE	Fool, the ones I'm wearing only cost two and nine three.
SEAGOON	Curse, I've failed. Very well, another offer. Give these man back their choppers and we'll see you get a fair trial, shot dead, strangled and set free.
DR. LONDONGLE	No.
SEAGOON	Why not?
DR. LONDONGLE	You might be lying, and it sounds risky.
SEAGOON	Then ying tong iddle i po.
DR. LONDONGLE	Never — never ying tong iddle i po. No, gentlemen, I'll not be forestalled now. I'm too near my goal.
F.X.	**FOOTBALL WHISTLE.**
BLUEBOTTLE	Off side, he's too near his own goal.
SEAGOON	Shut up.
BLUEBOTTLE	Shut up.
ECCLES	Shut up, Eccles.
SEAGOON	Shut up, Eccles.
BLUEBOTTLE	Shunt unpe, Enkles.
OMNES	Shut up, etc. . . .
MORIARTY	Helpp! — who's turned out the light — who's turned the light out?
DR. LONDONGLE	It's me, ha ha.
SEAGOON	Economical devil, trying to save electricity, eh? O'Brien?
O'BRIEN	Yeah? Begorrah mate.

SEAGOON	Put on this invisible beard — creep up on the light switch and while it can't see you — switch it on!
O'BRIEN	Okay — begorrah . . . *(Off)* Okay, it's on.
SEAGOON	Huzah. Right men, open your eyes, the light's on.
BLOODNOK	Ohhh — look at Dr. Londongler — he's gone.
SEAGOON	Don't worry, he won't get far in those cheap woollen bloomers — there's frost about. In any case, the moment he steps outside this castle the wolves are bound to get him.
BLOODNOK	Why?
SEAGOON	*(dry)* They're looking for a new goal-keeper.
MORIARTY	Stop those crazy carefully-rehearsed ad libs.
SEAGOON	Men, to catch this Dr. Londongler won't be easy — he's clever. We're going to need brains.
ECCLES	*(pause)* Well, I'll go and make the tea.
GRAMS	HORSE & CARRIAGE DOWN IN COBBLED COURTYARD STARTS OFF AT A GALLOP.
BLOODNOK	Ohh, great scorched gringes — down there! Londongler's escaping.
SEAGOON	Where?
BLOODNOK	There — stick your head out the window.
GRAMS	HEAD BEING STUFFED THROUGH GLASS WINDOW. BREAKING GLASS.
BLOODNOK	Bandage?
SEAGOON	No thanks.
BLOODNOK	But you're bleeding awful.
SEAGOON	Give me the bandage. O'Brien? Lay out my leaving-the-castle-suit. Men — after him — one two —
OMNES	*(fast) (sing)* On through the hail, like a pack of hungry wolves on the trail, we are after you, dead or alive — we are out to get you, dead or alive.
F.X.	MARCHING BOX.
ORCHESTRA	CHORDS TO SUGGEST BEGINNING OF A GREAT ADVENTURE (MACABRE).
BILL	With a small stove, Lord Seagoon set off in hot pursuit in his horse-drawn motor car. The trail of missing teeth led them to the village of Tarzan Call. And there, next to a newsvendor's shop in which this week's copy of the Radio Times is now on sale — they stopped.
SEAGOON	All out now, men — it looks like he's in this Café Filthmuck.
GRYTPYPE-THYNNE	Yes — I think there's something funny going on inside.
SEAGOON	Why?

GRYTPYPE-THYNNE	I can hear somebody laughing.
SEAGOON	Follow me in, men.
F.X.	DOOR OPENS. SOUND OF A BEER GARDEN. DISTANT ZITHER.
SEAGOON	Now, we don't want to look suspicious so put your coats over your heads and crawl nonchalantly across the floor on your backs. And keep your Union Jacks down. Follow me. Ughh — this is fooling them. Ughhh.
PETER	(Flowerdew-raving) 'Ere — you lot on the floor — hurry up, we're waiting to dance. Makes you spit.
SEAGOON	I'm sorry, madame — we are looking for escaped miniature convicts, but apparently they're out of season. Eccles?
ECCLES	Yer?
SEAGOON	Shut up.
ECCLES	Shut up.
SEAGOON	Eccles?
ECCLES	Yer?
F.X.	PISTOL SHOT.
ECCLES	Thank you.
ORCHESTRA	ROLL ON DRUM AND CYMBAL CRASH.
DR. LONDONGLE	(announcing a little off) Mein lieber damunherren —
SEAGOON	Look — it's Londongler!
DR. LONDONGLE	Presenting the cabaret — that queen of reeking Spanish dancers — Señorita Gladys la Tigernutta — my fiancée, with her fifty steaming castanet dancers.
GRAMS	FLAMENCO MUSIC AND CASTANETS.
SEAGOON	Keep calm, men. Let's see what happens.
GRYTPYPE-THYNNE	Look, the black's coming off the castanets.
SEAGOON	Yes — they're white underneath. Could they be what the listeners have known all along?
MORIARTY	It's our teeth — teeethhhhhh.
OMNES	(Shouts of 'Teeth' 'Teeth')
F.X.	SNAPPING OF TEETH.
ORCHESTRA	MUSIC UP AND OUT.
SEAGOON	And that, folks, is how we found Londongler's missing teeth horde — we never found him, and I often wonder if he ever continued his teeth activities.
BILL	(no teeth) You've been listening to The Goon Show.

ORCHESTRA	**SIGNATURE TUNE: UP AND DOWN FOR:—**
BILL	That was The Goon Show — a BBC recorded programme featuring Peter Sellers, Harry Secombe, Spike Milligan and Valentine Dyall with the Ray Ellington Quartet and Max Geldray. The orchestra was conducted by Wally Stott. Script by Spike Milligan. Announcer: Wallace Greenslade. The programme was produced by Peter Eton.
ORCHESTRA	**SIGNATURE TUNE UP TO END.**
	(Applause)
MAX & ORCHESTRA	**'CRAZY RHYTHM' PLAYOUT.**

BACKWORD
HARRY SECOMBE

And this is where the story *really* starts. . . .

I wonder how many people realise how near we have become in real life to the characters we played. Scratch Peter and you find Bluebottle. Discard the trappings of the jet set and there he is—querulous in his Mum's old drawers, thinking lecherous thoughts about Gladys Twit and wearing boxing gloves to bed. Eccles lurks behind Spike's every move, liable to pop out at the most unlikely moments. A serious discussion about conservation can degenerate in seconds to absurdity by a sudden raising and lowering of the eyebrows and the sublime idiocy of the famous Eccles remark 'Having a good time?'. Spike thinks of me as Neddie. No matter what I do or to whatever theatrical or social aspirations I may pretend he can see that beneath the finger-nail-deep veneer of sophistication there lie the shattered underpants and the tattered vest emblazoned with the Union Jack of Neddie Seagoon, playboy of the Western Mail.

Regardless of how we saw ourselves, the gentlemen of the Press were never quite sure how to describe us. They called us 'the angry young men of comedy'; they saw in the show overtones of Kafka, Ionesco, even Dylan Thomas; they compared us to the Marx Brothers; we were praised over-fulsomely by some, and condemned out of hand as incoherent idiots by others.

But for we three the Goon Show was a chance to get together on a Sunday and indulge in our private fantasies. It was a time for hysteria and brandy, for soaring upward on the thermal currents of Milligan's imagination, a time for wishing every day of the week to be a Sunday.

Harry Sleeping
by Spike

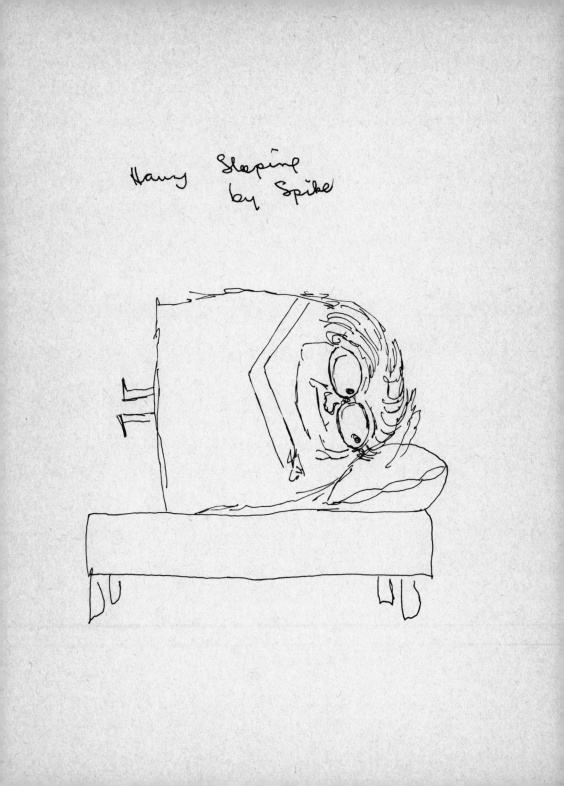